THE TABOR OPERA HOUSE:
A CAPTIVATING HISTORY

By

Evelyn E. Livingston Furman

FIRST PRINTING

LIBRARY OF CONGRESS CATALOG CARD NUMBER: 72-88027
MANUFACTURED IN THE UNITED STATES OF AMERICA

" - - - all the good the past hath had
        Remains to make our own time glad. - - - "

John Greenleaf Whittier

"May this old show house rise to heights supernal;
As each year turns its soiled and blotted page;
Built on these mountain tops that stand eternal;
Let hope as well as memory light its stage."

"The Tabor Opera House" poem
by Frank E. Vaugn, Leadville
poet and newspaperman.

ANECDOTES FROM AN OCTOBER 8, 1905 PLAYBILL:

"Children in arms positively not admitted to theatre."

"The numerous complaints have forced the management to adopt a rule in regard to late comers, and such cannot be seated while curtain is up."

FROM THE BILL OF PLAY FOR "THE PIT":

"The management requests that ladies will kindly not wear their hats in any part of the theatre."

"If the play pleases you, show your appreciation. The players like it, and it urges them to do their best."

"Read the advertisements in this program closely and profit thereby."

"Ladies having in charge children who become noisy will be expected to promptly remove them from the theatre."

H.A.W. TABOR

AUGUSTA TABOR
Photo courtesy of the Denver Public Library Western Collection.

THE STORY OF H. A. W. TABOR

and

THE TABOR TRIANGLE

A history of the Tabor Opera House in Leadville, Colorado cannot exist without the stories of its illustrious builder, H.A. W. Tabor, and "The Tabor Triangle". . . .

And this is the chronicle of the man who made a fortune in mining with unbelievable rapidity. Seemingly, for a time, almost everything Tabor touched turned to gold! Then, with another spin of Fortune's wheel, the wealth was gone, almost as swiftly.

H.A.W. Tabor was estimated, at that time, to be worth at least ten million dollars, although newspaper accounts of his day set the figure at twenty million dollars. How Tabor disbursed this enormous amount is a fascinating story in itself. For, undoubtedly, he believed that money prevailed only to be spent. Thus, he spent his millions and continued spending as if there would be no end to the outpouring of wealth from his mines. In fact, his expenditures made front-page newspaper copy as far away as Chicago and New York. Moreover, Tabor's fame soon spread around the world.

But, let's journey back into the past to *before* "The Tabor Triangle" originated:

Of English ancestry, Horace Austin Warner Tabor was born in Orleans County, Vermont on November 26, 1830. His parents were poor, so he had no educational advantages. Most of his knowledge was gained by observation and experience. Tabor was a stone-cutter, a trade which he followed until he was 25 years old. Later, in Maine, he worked for the father of Augusta Pierce, a young lady whom he married in 1857.

Horace Tabor took his new bride to Kansas where they intended to try farming for a few years. The trip enroute was long and difficult, but they finally reached their destination.

"Here we are, Augusta," said Horace Tabor, as the oxen brought the covered wagon to a grinding halt.

Horace hurried about the wagon, but stopped long enough to help his new bride down onto Kansas soil, their new homestead. Two men had accompanied the Tabors on the trip, and had helped in many ways on the long journey. (The pioneers usually traveled in groups, believing there was "safety in numbers.")

"I do believe the wind is blowing even harder than before," commented Augusta, holding tightly onto her bonnet.

For as far as Augusta and Horace could see, there was nothing but open prairie. There were no buildings around except for a 12' x 16' cabin they were to now call home.

"Here's our 160 acres," said Horace, swinging his arms in the direction of their farm.

Despite the dust, blown by the wind, everyone smiled, and prepared to unload the wagon.

Augusta's heart ached, as she tried to adjust herself to the thought of living in this new country. What a comfortable home she had left in Augusta, Maine! Her mother and father would be shocked if they could see their daughter now, covered with Kansas dust.

(From Augusta, Maine, the couple had traveled to St. Louis, Missouri, which was the end of the railroad. Then a five-day boat trip brought them to Kansas City, where they purchased a yoke of oxen, a wagon, new farming tools, and some seeds before heading on west.)

"Well," said Augusta, "I must see what I can do, now that we are here."

She stepped inside the cabin, and saw a cook stove, a dilapidated trunk, and a rough bedstead made of poles, upon which was a bed tick filled with prairie grass.

"Oh dear," Augusta said, to herself, dejectedly. "How can I ever live here?" She sat down on the trunk and cried!

"There, there!" soothed Horace in a low tone, as he carried in an armload of supplies from the wagon. "Everything's going to be all right," he assured her, trying to comfort her as best he could.

"I knew what it would be like here," sobbed Augusta. "But I just can't help feeling this way."

The other two men couldn't stand tears, so they busied themselves outside, no doubt hoping she wouldn't get too homesick.

Augusta was brave, and soon brushed away her tears. She unpacked the belongings, and to the best of her ability, tried to put everything in order. Everyone was hungry, and Augusta soon had a meal prepared which they eagerly devoured. Subsequently, the two men took rooms nearby, and these boarders helped support the Tabors.

Excited about his farming, Horace went to work diligently, tilling the soil and sowing the seed. Afterwards, Augusta and Horace stood looking proudly out across the newly-planted fields. And later, Augusta helped in the fields also, after finishing her household tasks.

There was no rain all summer. So much hard work, and no harvest!

"What are we going to do?" asked Augusta.

"I'm going to Fort Riley, and work as a stone-cutter," announced Horace. "There's a lot of new building going on there, and workmen are wanted."

While Horace was in Fort Riley, Augusta was busy with her small baby Maxcy, and raised chickens to make a little money, also. There were many Indians in the territory, causing Augusta much worry. The numerous rattlesnakes terrified her, too, and she could not keep them out of the cabin for they crawled inside, seeking shade. Augusta found that the only safe place to sit was on a three-legged stool—with her feet tucked under her.

The next year, the Tabors were encouraged for they had an abundant crop. But alas! There was no market for it.

"Oh, Horace," Augusta exclaimed, "What can we do? Eggs are only 3c per dozen!" "Oh, well," she finally concluded, "I still have my boarders, and I can also sell some of my butter."

Early-day Leadville prospector, Circa 1859-1860.

California Gulch, where Abe Lee made the first gold discovery.

Lumber train of mules, ready to start for the high places near Leadville. Note the long lengths of lumber tied to each mule.

Interior of spacious log cabin near Leadville, Circa 1880. Men's identity unknown.

Sketch of the early Leadville, before honored with a name.

Leadville in its infancy. View of the Embryo City, from Brooklyn Heights.

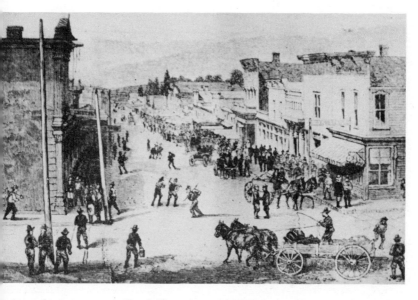

nimated street scene in Leadville, winter of 1878-9. Looking west down lower
bestnut Street, Tabor's Bank is in left foreground.

Early-day Leadville, Colo., from Capitol Hill.

Winter's morning, Leadville. On horizon, left to right, are Mounts Elber. French, and Massive.

Harrison Ave., 1879, Leadville, Colo.

West side of Harrison Ave., Leadville, Colo.

State Street, Leadville, Colo.

13

In addition to farming, Horace Tabor took an active part in the then-storm political events in Kansas. He was a member of the Kansas Legislature when tha body was forcibly dispersed by an order of the United States President, Frankli Pierce.

Then one day came a sudden turn of events! News of the sensational Pikes Pea gold rush reached the ears of the Tabors. Attracted by this excitement, Horac Tabor decided to try his luck in the new "El Dorado." He realized the grea hardships ahead, and suggested to Augusta that she might be better off to go hom to Maine.

"No, no, Horace! My place is with you," Augusta refused.

In 1859, those brave pioneers crossed the plains of Kansas and Colorado i prairie schooners. Filled with new hope, they again endured innumerable hard ships on their journey towards "El Dorado." There were no roads; and most the way they had no fuel, making it difficult for Augusta to cook a meal. Indian followed them all the way. Though friendly, the redskins continually begged an pilfered.

Haggard and worn, the travelers finally arrived in Denver, where they spent th winter. Horace Tabor started his search for gold in this region until sprin arrived, while Augusta went about her usual duties and was busy with the care their son, Maxcy, who was ill.

In the spring, they started for California Gulch, a very difficult journey throug the mountains. Abe Lee had just made his rich discovery in Californ Gulch before the arrival of the Tabors. Tabor joined in and staked his claim. Th season, his prospecting and mining brought him $5,000. However, cold weath made it impossible to continue mining until the next spring.

The Tabors opened up a general merchandise store in a new settlement nam Oro; and myriad cabins extended as far as the town of Malta.

At the end of the second season, Mr. Tabor had reaped $15,000. When th gold excitement dwindled, and new discoveries were made over the mounta range in Buckskin Joe, Horace Tabor followed the shifting population there, a opened an even larger and better-stocked store than the one in Oro.

Some years later, Oro again showed signs of activity; and the result was t second great mining discovery. Back to Oro went the Tabors with their stor Eventually, the population moved a little northward, and thus, the new city call Leadville was born.

When he was sure this was the real bonanza, Tabor moved the store and p office once again. He was the postmaster, and also the first mayor of Leadville. I was also re-elected as the second mayor of this fast-growing city, and tried to bri form and order where there had been chaos in this wild mountainous frontier.

The Tabor name in those early days was known to almost everyone. Peop from miles around came to the Tabor store for their groceries and suppli Augusta Tabor never turned away anyone not having money. Many a p prospector was grubstaked by Horace Tabor. Always too generous for his ov good, Tabor carried thousands of dollars on his ledgers which he never collect

The Tabors lived, for a time, in a small clapboard cottage on Harrison Avenu Later, Tabor moved this house to Carbonate Avenue to make way for the Tal Opera House. Harrison Avenue was fast becoming the new business distri

14

Chestnut was the main street of Leadville in the early days, and State Street was the next street north. These streets were crowded with dance halls, variety theaters, and various other businesses.

Carbonate Avenue was just above State Street, east of Harrison Avenue and was lined with the dwellings of merchant princes, and important mining men of Leadville. Capitol Hill was another fashionable quarter. Space here was set aside for future State buildings. Optimistic citizens felt that the "Magic City" was destined to become the capitol of Colorado. The houses on Capitol Hill were of imposing architecture, having more than four angles, ornamental cornices, and were even painted!

Tabor had never given up his search for gold, and now the results were soon to amaze the entire world. One day, two shoemakers named August Rische and George Hook came to Tabor for aid. This was one time that grubstaking "paid off" for Horace Tabor. He invested $60 in outfitting these two men in their search for gold. They continued their work on Fryer Hill, and eventually found the Little Pittsburgh. The known vein, already discovered, would require sinking a shaft to a depth of 500 feet. Not so with these two lucky fellows. They struck bonanza at a depth of only 28 feet! This great strike resulted in a mine that was, in but a mere week's time, producing at the rate of $8,000 per week. Both Mr. Hook and Mr. Rische sold out; and Mr. Tabor cleared between a million and a million and a half dollars from the property.

Soon, he began to develop more mining properties. He bought the Matchless, a silver mine, for $117,000. He had large interests, too, in many other mines such as the Scooper, Dunkin, Chrysolite, Union Emma, Empire, Denver City, Henriett, Maid of Erin, Hibernia, and the May Queen. Many other enterprises followed, such as the Tabor Milling Company. He invested heavily in areas outside of Leadville, and even in foreign countries, as well.

"Chicken Bill," a notorious mining-camp "character" owned a mining property which he was anxious to sell. He had mined down for 75 feet, and still hadn't found any mineral. Stealing some rich ore from Mr. Tabor's own Chrysolite bins, he then showed Mr. Tabor the assay report. Mr. Tabor investigated, and thought it a good proposition, so "Chicken Bill" promptly sold his worthless mine to Mr. Tabor.

Tabor's workmen soon reported that they could find nothing of value in this good-for-nothing mine. "Go ahead and sink further down, anyway," Tabor ordered. Lo and behold! After the shaft went down only three more feet, they struck a very rich pocket of ore! Thus, Mr. Tabor earned several more million dollars! Fortune was definitely on Mr. Tabor's side, and the swindle which "Chicken Bill" had intended for his victim turned out to be a real bonanza.

With this vast accumulation of wealth, Horace Tabor set out to build Leadville into a great city. He supplied a gas works, water works, a fire department, and a cavalry company. He donated to the churches, schools, hospitals, and to any worthy cause. He built the Tabor Opera House, and helped build the Clarendon Hotel. Additionally, he completed the construction of the Tabor Grand Hotel; organized a telephone company; founded the Bank of Leadville; and owned a newspaper. Tabor often said, "I'm going to make Leadville a first-class city, so people will want to stay here!"

15

Theodore Hook, discoverer of the Little Pittsburgh Mine.

August Rische, mining associate Theodore Hook.

The Little Pittsburgh Mine, Leadville, Colo.

16

The Chrysolite Mine, Leadville, Colo.

The Denver City Mine, Leadville, Colo.

17

Leonard Shaft of the Matchless Mine, Leadville, Colo.

Photo of an original Matchless Mine painting. From the Florence A. Holliste collection.

Grand Hotel on Chestnut St., Leadville, Colo.

Thomas F. Walsh, pioneer proprietor of the Grand Hotel, Leadville.

C.W. Kitchen, one-time proprietor of the Hotel Kitchen, later named the Tabor Grand Hotel.

Page reproduction from the Tabor Grand Hotel Register.

Page reproduction from the Tabor Grand Hotel Register. Note H.A.W. Tabor's signature on this page.

Page reproduction from the Tabor Grand Hotel Register. Note P.D. McCourt signature on this page. McCourt was Baby Doe Tabor's brother.

22

THE TABOR GRAND.

LEADVILLE, COLO.

GEO. R. FISHER

NAME	RESIDENCE	TIME	ROOMS
Sunday October 11th 1876			
W. Gregory	Pueblo	13	44
Robt. Coleman	Buena Vista	"	
		"	
J. Ly. Hawkins Jr	City	5	
K. Schoenstein		5	
E. H. Taylor	Redcliff	5	24
H. Williams	Denver	"	
C. P. Hoyt		"	
Chas. Cavendish	with Parents	"	
E. F. Brace	Leavenworth	5	67
Mrs. H. Halloran	St. Louis	5	68
Geo. A. Daly	Dalys Vacation Co.	8	16
Wm. Daly Jr & Wife	" "	"	44
Robert Daly	Part of	"	54
Chas. R. Brooks		"	47
Daniel Daly	Dalys Vacation Co	"	47
Chas Lorenberg	"	"	34
Geo. W. Derires	"	"	46
Harry L. Dick	"	"	46
E. F. Morrigan	"	"	20
Mrs. Bloodgood	"	"	35
Miss Conway	"	"	35
Frank Nicholson	St. Louis	"	45
		"	22
J. W. Herbert	Denver	"	02
A. W. Beed	Do	"	17
Friday	Pueblo	2	56
I. R. French	St. Joe Mo	"	33
J. R. Rucker	City	"	6

Page reproduction from the Tabor Grand Hotel Register.

23

Page reproduction from the Tabor Grand Hotel Register. Again, note Tabor's signature.

Home of Augusta Tabor, 17th & Broadway, Denver, Photo by W.H. Jackson, from the Denver Public Library Western Collection.

H.A.W. Tabor residence at 13th & Sherman Streets, Denver. From the Denver Public Library Western Collection.

Ore wagon enroute from Leadville. Photo courtesy of Olivia Reichle.

Leadville people heading for a "Tally-Ho" picnic. Photo courtesy of Olivia Reichle.

Circumstances might have been very different in Leadville today had not the great H.A.W. Tabor been willing to spend his own money for the benefit of many. This lavish spending resulted in an eminent city that would thrive on and on. No man ever did more for Leadville or Colorado than did H.A.W. Tabor!

In 1880, the Tabors moved to Denver. Horace Tabor did much upbuilding of Denver, deciding to make this Queen City the showplace of the West. Property sky-rocketed in price as soon as Mr. Tabor started buying and building.

By 1860, Denver had been a frontier town. Early-day pioneers stopped here to rest and gather provisions and supplies before going elsewhere in their search for gold, though some remained to operate various businesses. There were no substantial buildings in 1860 except for the Broadwell Hotel at Larimer and 16th Streets.

When Mr. Tabor, in 1880, returned to Denver with his fortune, he purchased the Broadwell corner, and started to build extensively. On the site of the old Broadwell House, he built the Tabor Building, the first structure in Denver to be made of dressed stone, and it also had the distinction of being the first to rise above four stories high. At 16th and Curtis Streets, in 1880-1881, Tabor built the great Tabor Grand Opera House, constructed of red pressed brick and trimmed with light sandstone. He also bought a mansion on Broadway; later he owned a mansion at 13th and Sherman Streets. At 15th and Cleveland Place stood the Metropolitan Theater, built in 1889; and when in 1892 it burned, leaving nothing but its granite walls, the theater was owned by H.A.W. Tabor. Mr. Tabor also bought half of the stock in the First National Bank of Denver, and also purchased one-fourth interest in Borden Tabor and Company. Together with Marshall Field of Chicago, he acquired possessions that likewise yielded millions.

Horace Tabor poured money into politics, supporting the Republican Party almost single-handedly. He was Lieutenant Governor of Colorado from 1879 to 1883; and served as United States Senator for a thirty-day term in 1883 to fill a vacancy. Mr. Tabor was chairman of the State Central Committee, and conducted the Republican campaign of 1886 with success. In 1891, he was chosen president of the Denver Chamber of Commerce and Board of Trade.

After the Tabors moved to Denver, they drifted apart. Mr. Tabor, extremely occupied with business matters, saw less and less of Augusta. But more importantly, someone else had captured his attention: A beautiful blonde named Elizabeth McCourt appeared on the scene. A divorce followed, leaving Augusta heartbroken and alone. She had not wanted the divorce. "Against my will," she cried, crushed and broken.

Augusta remained alone in the Broadway mansion, and received a good portion of the Tabor fortune in the divorce settlement. The scandal of the divorce, and Mr. Tabor's later marriage to Elizabeth McCourt in 1883, put an end to Mr. Tabor's political ambitions.

Elizabeth McCourt, born in 1854, was from Oshkosh, Wisconsin. She was one of a large family, and her father was a tailor. Possessing remarkable beauty, she was known as the "Belle of Oshkosh." She married Harvey Doe, and they set out for the West to seek their fortune. They settled in Central City, Colorado, and for a few years, they worked at mining, but their venture was not successful. Later, Elizabeth and Harvey were divorced.

Baby Doe, as Elizabeth was nicknamed in Central City, was left without funds. Nonetheless, she decided she wanted to go to Leadville, where everything was booming. Jake Sands, a friend of hers who had been in business in Central City, had just moved his clothing store to Leadville, occupying the north section of the ground floor in the Tabor Opera House. So it was Jake Sands who aided her in getting to Leadville.

Shortly after Baby Doe arrived in Leadville, someone pointed out the wealthy Horace Tabor to her, and she immediately "set her cap" for him. She had a chance to observe him in a hotel lobby, as he stood talking to his mining friends congregated there. They were discussing the latest mining news of the day, with great excitement.

Although middle-aged and slightly stoop-shouldered from hard work, Tabor looked very distinguished to the former Belle of Oshkosh. Dressed in a dark suit and with magnificent cuff buttons sparkling with diamonds and onyx, he was a striking fellow, thought Baby Doe, watching him. A large diamong ring on his finger flashed in the light as he nervously pulled, once, at his black mustache. Tabor smoothed back his black hair as he held his stove-pipe hat in his hands. He kept turning his hat round and round, as the conversation continued. Baby Doe sensed a certain magic power in this man Tabor!

As most of the men were leaving the building, Baby Doe overheard their conversation drift to talk of the evening's attraction at the Tabor Opera House, and it was almost show-time.

After the show, many people went to the Saddle Rock Restaurant near the Tabor Opera House, where Baby Doe was finally clever enough to meet Mr. Tabor. She had dreamed of this meeting for days, an event which was to change the course of her entire life.

From the first, Horace and Baby Doe were attracted to each other. Not only was he the richest man around, but he also fascinated her. There was a look of honesty underneath his rugged features. He had a generous and charitable manner that Baby Doe liked.

So it was that Baby Doe entered into H.A.W. Tabor's life, and thus, "The Tabor Triangle" was born. Many persons thought the beautiful Baby Doe was only after Tabor's money. Augusta, his hardworking first wife, had the sympathy of everyone. She didn't care for the glamour that wealth could bring. But Baby Doe, like Mr. Tabor, loved all the wonderful things which great fortune could supply.

Mr. Tabor, as U.S. Senator, had arranged a very elaborate and fashionable wedding to Baby Doe on March 1, 1883 in the Willard Hotel in Washington, D.C. The bride wore a $7,000 wedding outfit. President Chester Arthur and his Cabinet were in attendance. But the women invited, refused to attend, except for Baby Doe's relatives, and Baby Doe never was accepted into society.

After the Washington wedding, Horace and Baby Doe Tabor made their first home in the Windsor Hotel in Denver. Later, they moved to a fine mansion at 13th and Sherman Streets. Two children were born to them. The first was named Elizabeth Bonduel Lillie, and the other, Rosemary Echo Silver Dollar. Lillie's christening outfit cost $15,000 and she was featured in Harper's Bazaar as the most famous of babies. The Tabors lavished the most expensive items on their offspring, while society continued to snub Baby Doe.

Left is the three-story Tabor Opera House. Next door is the Clarendon Hotel, Photo courtesy of The Denver Public Library Western Collection.

Tabor Opera House stage on opening night, November 20, 1879. The ornate Andrews opera chairs are silhouetted against the orchestra pit. Note H.A.W. Tabor's picture on easel at stage right. From Mrs. Theresa O'Brien collection.

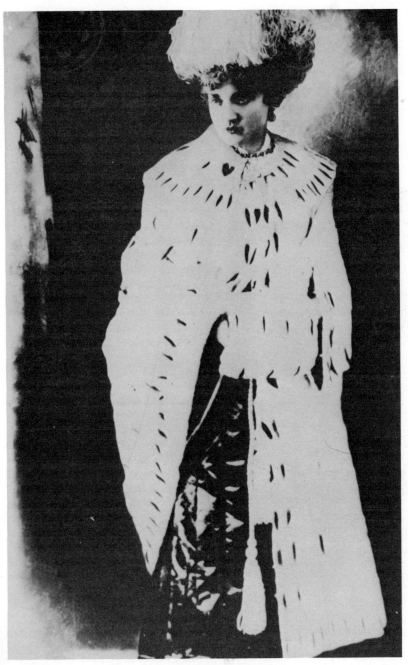

Baby Doe Tabor. From The Denver Public Library Western Collection. Courtesy of Caroline Bancroft.

Horace A. W. Tabor,

Lizzie Bonduel McCourt,

Married

Thursday, March first,

Eighteen hundred & eighty three.

Washington, D.C.

The Tabor-McCourt wedding invitation. From The Denver Public Library Western Collection.

H.A.W. Tabor and Baby Doe were married in this setting at the Hotel Willard, Washington, D.C., March 1, 1883. From The Denver Public Library Western Collection.

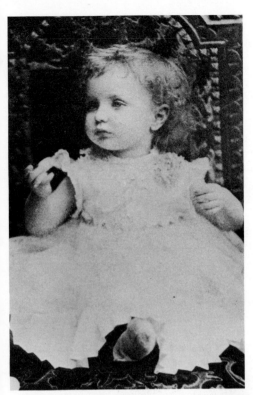

Baby Lillie Tabor. From The Denver Public Library Western Collection. Courtesy of Caroline Bancroft.

August 29, 1910—Silver Dollar Tabor meets President Theodore Roosevelt at a press club dinner. From The Denver Public Library Western Collection.

In the 1890's, the Tabor fortune dwindled and luxurious living was approaching an end. Horace Tabor fell heavily into debt, as the panic of 1893 hit him hard. Congress repealed the Sherman Silver Act, so the government was no longer in the market for silver. The price dropped from $1.29 to 50c per ounce, less than the cost of mining it. Horace Tabor, including many others, faced ruin. His vast mining interests, and all his other property seemed to slip through his fingers.

That cruel year of 1893, many persons predicted that Tabor's pretty young wife would now leave him. After all, his wealth was gone, and he was a man 63 years old! But, much to everyone's surprise, this wife he had married only ten years previous, *did not* desert him.

The Tabor Opera House in Leadville was said to be the last of Mr. Tabor's holdings. Finally, even this went into the hands of Judge A.S. Weston. There had been a great deal of sentiment connected with this building. The Opera House had been Tabor's first great possession after he struck it rich. Not only did Mr. Tabor have a special love for the Tabor Opera House, but also for the Tabor Suite, on the second floor of the building. This had been his last Leadville home. (Even after Tabor moved to Denver, he still regarded Leadville as his real home.) From his windows in the suite, he could see Mount Massive and the rest of the majestic mountain range. Then to the south was California Gulch, where the fabulous gold rush started!

Now everything was gone, sold under the hammer, to satisfy the mortgages. By the turn of Fortune's wheel, Tabor seemed to be right back where he started! Baby Doe had been willing to sell her jewels to raise money, but they, too, were now gone. The Tabors took up cheap lodging in Denver, and tried to adjust to a simple way of life.

Augusta had not remained in Denver, but made her home in Pasadena, California, where she died in 1895. Her son, Maxcy, brought her remains to Denver for burial. She was said to have a wealth of millions, and left her fortune to Maxcy. Augusta always had a good business head, and invested her money wisely. She had offered to help her ex-husband when he was down and out, but he refused her aid.

Augusta is buried in Riverside Cemetary—not in a family plot, but "alone" among the surrounding graves of strangers. A small, flat stone in the earth marks her grave. Alone in the last years of her life, and alone now in death!

In life, Augusta in her modest way, was never one for flamboyancy. And so it would seem that the simple grey granite marker would perhaps be all that she might want.

Augusta always carried the torch for Mr. Tabor, hoping someday he would come back to her. She held ever in her memory the hardships and disappointments of the early pioneer life she had shared with her husband. Even though she was a frail woman, she shouldered more than her share of the responsibilities. Had she not always tried to remain at Tabor's side, he might not have attained the place in life he once held.

Augusta was the first white woman to arrive in California Gulch, a settlement which eventually resulted in what is now the town of Leadville. There was many a sick miner she nursed back to health. She fed a multitude of wayfaring strangers who were withou. means. Loved by everyone sho knew her, she is remembered for her excellent cooking and baking; and she took in many boarders.

Everyone mourned at the sad news of Augusta's death. Some folks say she died of a broken heart. She was rightfully called ''Leadville's First Lady.''

When the end of Mr. Tabor's fortune came, he accepted it bravely. As always, he was never discouraged. No matter how dark the future looked, he would try again!

1897 found Tabor once more working with his pick and shovel. He was never afraid of hard work. He wrote to a friend in Leadville saying he was working underground every day, and expressed confidence that everything would turn out all right. Horace Tabor had grubstaked many prospectors in the past, and had given so generously to others all his life. If only he could have been offered a little help now, in his poverty. There were those who had made millions but kept it for their own use.

The usual trend was for everyone to return to the eastern homes, and sit back and enjoy life in luxury. Not so with H.A.W. Tabor! He was at his wit's end trying to raise money to make a come-back in mining, and even prospected at Cripple Creek and elsewhere.

He finally discovered what appeared to be a valuable property in Boulder. Seeking funds to develop this, he appealed one day to Winfield Scott Stratton, the Cripple Creek millionaire. Tabor did not want a loan or gratuity, but only wanted Mr. Stratton to make an investment in this new venture. But Stratton evaded giving Tabor a direct answer.

Crestfallen, Tabor felt that no one cared, and his faith in mankind was almost destroyed. But later, that same evening, there appeared a ray of hope! For Mr. Stratton paid a visit to Mr. Tabor and handed him ten $1,000 bills. ''Make use of it as you want'' said Mr. Stratton, ''And if you can ever conveniently return it, do so. If not, don't consider there is any obligation in the matter.''

Horace Tabor might have been successful, but the money was gone before the ore in Boulder could be reached. Thus, Tabor was forced to quit that particular venture.

The Tabors were living in a few cheap rooms at the Windsor Hotel. Fate was to make this location their last home together. It was strange how, not long ago, they had started out anew here in this same hotel, only in a very elaborate suite! Here, Mr. Tabor had a magnificent view of the Rocky Mountains to the west and beyond that, the vivid memory of his beloved Leadville home.

Senator Wolcott came to the aid of Horace Tabor and used his influence concerning Tabor's appointment as Postmaster of Denver. President William McKinley, in response to the unanimous desire of the people, appointed Tabor to this position in 1898.

Tabor did not live long after his appointment as Postmaster of Denver. He was taken sick suddenly. As he grew steadily worse, a consultation by his physicians diagnosed his trouble as appendicitis. But they dared not operate due to his advanced age, and weakened condition. Baby Doe was with him at his bedside when he died April 10, 1899. She had faithfully stuck by her beloved husband until the end of his days. Also, at his bedside were Maxcy and the two daughters, Lillie, age 13, and Silver, age 9.

35

Thus, the curtain fell on the life of H.A.W. Tabor, ending one of the most fantastic and colorful American sagas. Not only did his life leave its mark on Leadville and Denver, but on the world as well. His beginning was at the foot of the ladder. Led by great determination, he reached the top.

The day Tabor was buried, flags were flown at half-mast throughout Colorado. His was the finest funeral ever held in Denver. Among the hundreds of floral tributes, the most outstanding one arrived from Leadville. Made of American Beauty roses, it was shaped in the form of a cornucopia. This creation was six feet high and most impressive, a touching last tribute from the people of Leadville to Postmaster Tabor! They had not forgotten, after all, how, in life, he had spilled out from his magic cornucopia an abundance of wealth for all of Leadville. That symbol will undoubtedly remain synonymous with the Horace Tabor mystique for years to come. Truly, he was the "Father of Leadville."

Baby Doe and her two daughters now faced life without their husband and father. For a time, they spent the winters in Denver. Eventually, Lillie, the older daughter, went to live in Wisconsin with Baby Doe's relatives, refusing to be associated with the Tabor name. She married, but little is known of her life thereafter.

Soon, Mrs. Baby Doe Tabor and Silver returned to Leadville to guard the Matchless Mine. For Tabor's dying words were: "Hang onto the Matchless! It will pay millions again."

The mother and daughter lived in a one-room shack near the mine. Silver, as a young girl, tried her hand at writing, but met with little success. Then she went to Chicago, where she died in 1925 in a cheap rooming house. Silver's tragic end came by alleged accidental scalding. Because of the suspicious circumstances surrounding her death, the world has always wondered about Silver. Baby Doe would never claim this was her daughter who died. "My Silver is safe in a convent," she insisted.

Stubbornly, Baby Doe continued living near the Matchless, to fulfill her husband's death wish. A few men tried to work the mine, but she never seemed to trust anyone.

Through the years, Baby Doe was faced with mortgages on the property. Finally, unknown to her, there came the foreclosure, but the new owners did not disturb her. Bravely, she continued guarding the Matchless with a shotgun, still waiting for the day when the mine would pay again.

She walked to Leadville, about a mile from her cabin, and picked up groceries and supplies, regularly. She was always anxious for her mail and often stopped by the library to read the newspapers.

A familiar but now pitiful-looking figure in Leadville, she dressed in old clothing wearing a worn black coat, a riding hat tied to her head with a scarf, and gunny sacks fastened around her feet.

Baby Doe had little money, but she was given some financial assistance by her brother, Peter McCourt, in Denver. He made arrangements with the Leadville grocerymen to let Baby Doe have whatever merchandise she wanted, promising that he would pay the bill. Since this business deal by her brother was made unbeknownst to her, she would say to the storekeepers as she took the groceries and supplies: "I'll pay you when the Matchless comes back." Baby Doe never would accept charity—she was just too proud.

The second Mrs. Tabor continued to live almost a hermit-like existance, but often visited her Leadville friends. Though strangers frequently knocked on her cabin door, she would not accept them, however, she would welcome her friends.

One day, two of Mrs. Tabor's ladyfriends walked up to her cabin to pay her a visit. After the usual greetings were exchanged, one of the ladies said to her, "It must be pretty lonesome for you up here all alone."

"Not at all," replied Mrs. Tabor. "I still have my memories."

"Now with everyone gone, it must be hard," said the other friend.

Even the man living down the hill from Baby Doe who had chopped her wood and carried her water was dead now. But there was still quite an ample supply of wood piled up on the outside wall of the cabin. "I'll make this last through the winter," said Mrs. Tabor, carrying in a few sticks and laying them carefully by the stove. "The coal supply around in back is running out, but I'll soon have another load up here," continued Baby Doe.

The conversation shifted to the subject of mining, which did not interest her two lady friends. "There's a touch of fall in the air," said one friend, as the three women stood looking out the cabin window over Leadville.

Before the ladies departed, Baby Doe accompanied them in a walk near the Matchless shaft, and one of the ladies took a picture of Baby Doe and the other friend. "Come again," said Baby Doe, afterwards, smiling at the two ladies, who soon disappeared behind a rocky dump, and on down the road.

Baby Doe sat down outside her cabin. Everything was still, except for the sound of the wind blowing through the swaying tops of the tall pine trees. She was thinking how she loved to walk among those trees; to smell the pleasant pungent scent of the pines; to hear the fallen and dried pine needles crunch under her feet. Occasionally, a little chipmunk would dart across her path, or she would see a gopher disappearing down a nearby hole. There were always the camprobbers near her cabin and a few bluejays in the distance to keep her company.

The days had grown short and the sun would soon be setting. She remembered she had a new supply of groceries. "How nice of the grocery boy to give me a ride home again today," thought Baby Doe. "I'm past 80 years old and those walks are getting mighty hard for me!" She also thought of the better days when she proudly wore the most fashionable and expensive shoes of the day, instead of the ugly gunny sacks which now encased her feet for warmth.

With slow steps, Baby Doe trudged into the cabin. "I must poke up the fire a bit," she said to herself.

Presently, the wood in the stove was crackling briskly, and the teakettle was boiling. Baby Doe reached up on the shelf to get her teacup and gently placed it before her to make tea. Next, she placed the old toaster (which she kept hanging on the wall) on top of the stove, and then toasted a slice of bread to perfection.

"Time to light the lamp," thought Baby Doe. She stepped over to the table and lit her lamp, turning it down very low and the wooden floorboards creaked under her feet as she moved about.

Sighing, she sat down in the old rocking chair. In the flickering lamplight, shadows crossed the room, as she rocked away, alone with her memories, in the old rocking chair. Comforted by the warmth from the nearby stove, she soon began to get drowsy.

Baby Doe Tabor in front of her cabin at the Matchless with Deck Wilmouth, a geologist in a placer mining venture in California Gulch. Taken 1933.

Baby Doe Tabor, left, and an unidentified friend, right. The two women are perched on the ladder leading down into a shaft of The Matchless.

Evelyn E. Furman Collection

hortly after Baby Doe's death, her cabin was entered by vandals who maliciously
ansacked the contents in search of valuables. Eventually, almost everything
isappeared in the greedy hands of souvenir hunters. Later, the cabin was
estored, and today, it is a tourist attraction.

Vision of Abominations in Jerusalem

to their deserts will I judge them; and they shall know that I am Jehovah.

8 And it came to pass in the sixth year, in the sixth *month*, in the fifth *day* of the month, as I sat in my house, and the elders of Judah sat before me, that the hand of the Lord Jehovah fell there upon me. 2 Then I beheld, and, lo, a likeness as the appearance of fire; from the appearance of his loins and downward, fire; and from his loins and upward, as the appearance of brightness, ¹as it were glowing metal. 3 And he put forth the form of a hand, and took me by a lock of my head; and the Spirit lifted me up between earth and heaven, and brought me in the visions of God to Jerusalem, to the door of the gate of the inner *court* that looketh toward the north; where was the seat of the image of jealousy, which provoketh to jealousy. 4 And, behold, the glory of the God of Israel was there, according to the ²appearance that I saw in the plain.

5 Then said he unto me, Son of man, lift up thine eyes now the way toward the north. So I lifted up mine eyes the way toward the north, and behold, northward of the gate of the altar this image of jealousy in the entry. 6 And he said unto me, Son of man, seest thou what they do? even the great abominations that the house of Israel do commit here, ³that I should go far off from my sanctuary? But ⁴thou shalt again see yet other great abominations.

7 And he brought me to the door of the court; and when I looked, behold, a hole in the wall. 8 Then said he unto me, Son of man, dig now in the wall: and when I had digged in the wall, behold, a door. 9 And he said unto me, Go in, and see the wicked abominations that they do here. 10 So I went in and saw; and behold, every form of

¹ Or, *as amber to look upon*   ² Or, *vision*   ³ Or, *to get them far off*   ⁴ Or, *turn thee yet again, and thou shalt see greater abominations* So also in ver. 13, 15.

creeping things, and abominable beasts, and all the idols of the house of Israel, portrayed upon the wall round about. 11 And there stood before them seventy men of the elders of the house of Israel; and in the midst of them stood Jaazaniah the son of Shaphan, every man with his censer in his hand; and the odor of the cloud of incense went up. 12 Then said he unto me, Son of man, hast thou seen what the elders of the house of Israel do in the dark, every man in his chambers of imagery? for they say, Jehovah seeth us not; Jehovah hath forsaken the land. 13 He said also unto me, Thou shalt again see yet other great abominations which they do.

14 Then he brought me to the door of the gate of Jehovah's house which was toward the north; and behold, there sat the women weeping for Tammuz. 15 Then said he unto me, Hast thou seen *this*, O son of man? thou shalt again see yet greater abominations than these.

16 And he brought me into the inner court of Jehovah's house; and behold, at the door of the temple of Jehovah, between the porch and the altar, were about five and twenty men, with their backs toward the temple of Jehovah, and their faces toward the east; and they were worshipping the sun toward the east. 17 Then he said unto me, Hast thou seen *this*, O son of man? Is it a light thing to the house of Judah that they commit the abominations which they commit here? for they have filled the land with violence, and have turned again to provoke me to anger: and, lo, they put the branch to their nose. 18 Therefore will I also deal in wrath; mine eye shall not spare, neither will I have pity; and though they cry in mine ears with a loud voice, yet will I not hear them.

9 Then he cried in mine ears with a loud voice, saying, ¹Cause ye them that have charge over the city to draw near, every man with his

¹ Or, *Draw ye near that &c.*

These are reproductions of four pages in Baby Doe's Bible. The margin notations are hers. Evelyn E. Furman collection.

the son bear the iniquity of the father? When the son hath done that which is lawful and right, and hath kept all my statutes, and hath done them, he shall surely live. 20 The soul that sinneth, it shall die: the son shall not bear the iniquity of the father, neither shall the father bear the iniquity of the son; the righteousness of the righteous shall be upon him, and the wickedness of the wicked shall be upon him.

21 But if the wicked turn from all his sins that he hath committed, and keep all my statutes, and do that which is lawful and right, he shall surely live, he shall not die. 22 None of his transgressions that he hath committed shall be remembered against him: in his righteousness that he hath done he shall live. 23 Have I any pleasure in the death of the wicked? saith the Lord Jehovah; and not rather that he should return from his way, and live? 24 But when the righteous turneth away from his righteousness, and committeth iniquity, and doeth according to all the abominations that the wicked man doeth, shall he live? None of his righteous deeds that he hath done shall be remembered: in his trespass that he hath trespassed, and in his sin that he hath sinned, in them shall he die.

25 Yet ye say, The way of the Lord is not equal. Hear now, O house of Israel: Is not my way equal? are not your ways unequal? 26 When the righteous man turneth away from his righteousness, and committeth iniquity, ¹and dieth ²therein; ³in his iniquity that he hath done shall he die. 27 Again, when the wicked man turneth away from his wickedness that he hath committed, and doeth that which is lawful and right, he shall save his soul alive. 28 Because he considereth, and turneth away from all his transgressions that he hath committed, he shall surely live, he shall not die. 29 Yet saith the house of Israel, The way of the Lord is not equal. O house of Israel, are not my ways equal? are not your ways unequal? 30 Therefore I will judge you, O house of Israel, every one according to his ways, saith the Lord Jehovah. Return ye, and turn yourselves from all your transgressions; ⁴so iniquity shall not be your ⁵ruin. 31 Cast away from you all your transgressions, wherein ye have transgressed; and make you a new heart and a new spirit: for why will ye die, O house of Israel? 32 For I have no pleasure in the death of him that dieth, saith the Lord Jehovah: wherefore turn yourselves, and live.

19 Moreover, take thou up a lamentation for the princes of Israel, 2 and say, What was thy mother? A lioness: she couched among lions, in the midst of the young lions she nourished her whelps. 3 And she brought up one of her whelps: he became a young lion, and he learned to catch the prey; he devoured men. 4 The nations also heard of him; he was taken in their pit; and they brought him with hooks unto the land of Egypt. 5 Now when she saw that she had waited, and her hope was lost, then she took another of her whelps, and made him a young lion. 6 And he went up and down among the lions; he became a young lion, and he learned to catch the prey; he devoured men. 7 And he knew their ⁶palaces, and laid waste their cities; and the land was desolate, and the fulness thereof, because of the noise of his roaring. 8 Then the nations set against him on every side from the provinces; and they spread their net over him; he was taken in their pit. 9 And they put him in a cage with hooks, and brought him to the king of Babylon; they brought him into strongholds, that his voice should no more be heard upon the mountains of Israel.

¹ Or, he shall die   ² Or, because of it   ³ Or, for   ⁴ Or, so shall they not be a stumblingblock of iniquity unto you   ⁵ Heb. stumblingblock   ⁶ Or, widows

4 MATTHEW 4.10 — 5.15

Jesus retires to Galilee.   Calls the Four.   The Sermon on the Mount.   The Beatitudes

[handwritten notes in top margin]

¹worship me. 10 Then saith Jesus unto him, Get thee hence, Satan: for it is written, ²Thou shalt worship the Lord thy God, and him only shalt thou serve. 11 Then the devil leaveth him; and behold, angels came and ministered unto him. —

12 Now when he heard that John was delivered up, he withdrew into Galilee; 13 and leaving Nazareth, he came and dwelt in Capernaum, which is by the sea, in the borders of Zebulun and Naphtali: 14 that it might be fulfilled which was spoken through Isaiah the prophet, saying,

15 ³The land of Zebulun and the land of Naphtali,

⁴Toward the sea, beyond the Jordan,

Galilee of the ⁵Gentiles, ·

16 The people that sat in darkness
Saw a great light,
And to them that sat in the region and shadow of death,
To them did light spring up.

17 From that time began Jesus to preach, and to say, Repent ye; for the kingdom of heaven is at hand.

18 And walking by the sea of Galilee, he saw two brethren, Simon who is called Peter, and Andrew his brother, casting a net into the sea; for they were fishers. 19 And he saith unto them, Come ye after me, and I will make you fishers of men. 20 And they straightway left the nets, and followed him. 21 And going on from thence he saw two other brethren, ⁶James the *son* of Zebedee, and John his brother, in the boat with Zebedee their father, mending their nets; and he called them. 22 And they straightway left the boat and their father, and followed him.

23 And ⁷Jesus went about in all Galilee, teaching in their synagogues, and preaching the ⁸gospel of the kingdom, and healing all manner of disease and all manner

of sickness among the people. 24 And the report of him went forth into all Syria: and they brought unto him all that were sick, holden with divers diseases and torments, ⁹possessed with demons, and epileptic, and palsied; and he healed them. 25 And there followed him great multitudes from Galilee and Decapolis and Jerusalem and Judæa and *from* beyond the Jordan.

5 And seeing the multitudes, he went up into the mountain: and when he had sat down, his disciples came unto him: 2 and he opened his mouth and taught them, saying,

3 Blessed are the poor in spirit: for theirs is the kingdom of heaven.

4 ¹⁰Blessed are they that mourn: for they shall be comforted.

5 Blessed are the meek: for they shall inherit the earth.

6 Blessed are they that hunger and thirst after righteousness: for they shall be filled.

7 Blessed are the merciful: for they shall obtain mercy.

8 Blessed are the pure in heart: for they shall see God.

9 Blessed are the peacemakers: for they shall be called sons of God.

10 Blessed are they that have been persecuted for righteousness' sake: for theirs is the kingdom of heaven. 11 Blessed are ye when *men* shall reproach you, and persecute you, and say all manner of evil against you falsely, for my sake. 12 Rejoice, and be exceeding glad: for great is your reward in heaven: for so persecuted they the prophets that were before you.

13 Ye are the salt of the earth: but if the salt have lost its savor, wherewith shall it be salted? it is thenceforth good for nothing, but to be cast out and trodden under foot of men. 14 Ye are the light of the world. A city set on a hill cannot be hid. 15 Neither do *men* light a lamp, and put it under the bushel, but on

¹ See marginal note on ch. 2. 2.   ² Dt. vi. 13.
³ Is. ix. 1, 2.   ⁴ Gr. *The way of the sea.*   ⁵ Gr. *nations:* and so elsewhere.   ⁶ Or, *Jacob*   ⁷ Some ancient authorities read *he.*   ⁸ Or, *good tidings:* and so elsewhere.
⁹ Or, *demoniacs*   ¹⁰ Some ancient authorities transpose ver. 4 and 5.

6.23 — 7.18　　　　**MATTHEW**　　　　　**7**

Of the Inner Light, of Anxiety, of Judging Others.　　The Golden Rule

body shall be full of light. 23 But if thine eye be evil, thy whole body shall be full of darkness. If therefore the light that is in thee be darkness, how great is the darkness! 24 No man can serve two masters: for either he will hate the one, and love the other; or else he will hold to one, and despise the other. Ye cannot serve God and mammon. 25 Therefore I say unto you, Be not anxious for your life, what ye shall eat, or what ye shall drink; nor yet for your body, what ye shall put on. Is not the life more than the food, and the body than the raiment? 26 Behold the birds of the heaven, that they sow not, neither do they reap, nor gather into barns; and your heavenly Father feedeth them. Are not ye of much more value than they? 27 And which of you by being anxious can add one cubit unto ¹the measure of his life? 28 And why are ye anxious concerning raiment? Consider the lilies of the field, how they grow; they toil not, neither do they spin: 29 yet I say unto you, that even Solomon in all his glory was not arrayed like one of these. 30 But if God doth so clothe the grass of the field, which to-day is, and to-morrow is cast into the oven, *shall he* not much more *clothe* you, O ye of little faith? 31 Be not therefore anxious, saying, What shall we eat? or, What shall we drink? or, Wherewithal shall we be clothed? 32 For after all these things do the Gentiles seek; for your heavenly Father knoweth that ye have need of all these things. 33 But seek ye first his kingdom, and his righteousness; and all these things shall be added unto you. 34 Be not therefore anxious for the morrow: for the morrow will be anxious for itself. Sufficient unto the day is the evil thereof.

7 Judge not, that ye be not judged. 2 For with what judgment ye judge, ye shall be judged: and with what measure ye mete, it shall be measured unto you. 3 And

¹ Or, *his stature*

why beholdest thou the mote that is in thy brother's eye, but considerest not the beam that is in thine own eye? 4 Or how wilt thou say to thy brother, Let me cast out the mote out of thine eye; and lo, the beam is in thine own eye? 5 Thou hypocrite, cast out first the beam out of thine own eye; and then shalt thou see clearly to cast out the mote out of thy brother's eye.

6 Give not that which is holy unto the dogs, neither cast your pearls before the swine, lest haply they trample them under their feet, and turn and rend you.

7 Ask, and it shall be given you; seek, and ye shall find; knock, and it shall be opened unto you: 8 for every one that asketh receiveth; and he that seeketh findeth; and to him that knocketh it shall be opened. 9 Or what man is there of you, who, if his son shall ask him for a loaf, will give him a stone; 10 or if he shall ask for a fish, will give him a serpent? 11 If ye then, being evil, know how to give good gifts unto your children, how much more shall your Father who is in heaven give good things to them that ask him? 12 All things therefore whatsoever ye would that men should do unto you, even so do ye also unto them: for this is the law and the prophets.

13 Enter ye in by the narrow gate: for wide ²is the gate, and broad is the way, that leadeth to destruction, and many are they that enter in thereby. 14 ³For narrow is the gate, and straitened the way, that leadeth unto life, and few are they that find it.

15 Beware of false prophets, who come to you in sheep's clothing, but inwardly are ravening wolves. 16 By their fruits ye shall know them. Do *men* gather grapes of thorns, or figs of thistles? 17 Even so every good tree bringeth forth good fruit; but the corrupt tree bringeth forth evil fruit. 18 A good tree cannot

² Some ancient authorities omit *is the gate.* ³ Many ancient authorities read *How narrow is the gate, &c*

Bearing a forlorn-sounding remark in Baby Doe's handwriting, this envelope w̶ found among her possessions after her death. Seemingly, the statement sho̶ dramatic proof of the genuine loneliness she felt while living at The Matchle̶

The original of this drawing is from the Evelyn E. Furman Collection. Copies for sale made especially for the Tabor Opera House

Horace and Baby Doe's final resting place, Mount Olivet Cemetery, Denver.

Baby Doe dropped off to sleep several times, and finally awoke with a start! urely she heard footsteps. Startled, she arose and blew out the lamp, then quietly ept to the small window near the bolted door and lifted a corner of the curtain. here was nothing in sight. "Oh, well! I'll retire now anyway," she decided, smissing the footsteps from her mind.

There were nights when Baby Doe talked to people in the spirit world. Such sits were recorded on her wall calendar. "Isn't it strange?" asked Baby Doe to erself, "People just can't understand this!"

Baby Doe recorded her various dreams on scraps of paper. Taken from her own ndwriting, one such recorded dream follows:

'July 15, Thurs.—1920 I dreamed my mother, in fine black, sat at my left, nd an old woman at my right. In Missouri—Joces Hathway people were lancing. They all sat down and one took me—danced wonderful, floated almost hrough the air—dark clothes. I was so light and graceful with a long train vaving and floating—grand and wonderful."

Baby Doe also recorded the current events of her day, such as this passage, ken from her own handwriting as follows: "D--- was lying to me about the ase, and how terrible. I went to J--- tonight and found out all D--- said. He scared -- out, God help me!"

In 1935, the curtain fell on the final act of the Tabor story, when Baby Doe's e also passed into history. Though the date of her death is officially recorded as arch 7, 1935, her body was discovered one winter morning in the shack near e Matchless. A Leadville grocery boy probably was the last person to see her ve. Friends of Baby Doe's noticed that no smoke was coming from her chimney, d so became alarmed. Shoveling through heavy snowdrifts, the worried friends iched the cabin. There was no sign of activity so they broke in through a ndow. Once inside, they encountered the frozen body of Baby Doe. Her autiful violet eyes were closed forever, and her musical voice was never to be ard again.

The tragic ending of this famous woman, who had so loyally guarded the atchless Mine, spread around the country. Newspaper headlines told of her ath and retold her life story. Her beauty had faded through the years, but like orace Tabor, her determination lasted until the end. The once-beautiful blonde o came West so long ago, had now finished the last scene on life's stage.

No drama such as the fantastic Tabor story could ever have been imagined by most adept dreamer. This true story will live forever. Such different women re Augusta and Baby Doe! Yet, each in her own way loved Horace Tabor.

Thus, the famous and intriging members of "The Tabor Triangle"— orace . . . Augusta . . . Baby Doe— will continue to enthrall one and all.

AUTHOR'S NOTES

The story of the Tabors was shown in the film "Silver Dollar." The movie stars were Edward G. Robinson and Bebe Daniels. The world premiere was in 1933 at the Denver Tabor Opera House. This film depicted many 1879-1880 scenes of Leadville, Colorado. The original roll curtain from the Leadville Tabor Opera House was even taken to Denver for the occasion.

On the elegant and impressive curtain at the former Tabor Grand Opera House in Denver were the words of Charles Kingsley, taken from "Old and New," a parable. Lines taken from part of his verse and used were as follows: "So fleet the works of man, back to their earth again; Ancient and holy things fade like a dream."

When this Denver Opera House was razed, I thought of these words with a great deal of sentiment. How true they were! Not many of the old Tabor land marks remain today. In fact, everything H.A.W. Tabor built in Denver has been destroyed, as one by one, the beautiful and historical buildings were torn down.

One cold winter day early in 1955, two gentlemen asked to be admitted to the Tabor Opera House, in Leadville. They informed me that they had come here to gain inspiration to write an opera about the Tabors, and were introduced to me as Douglas Moore and John Latouche.

Obligingly, I admitted them through the stage door, warning them that the building was closed and thus not heated during the winter season. But, as they stepped onto the stage, they became so enchanted that they hardly noticed the cold.

The two men paused to observe the priceless, hand-painted scenery, as they walked to centerstage, and then halted. Standing there, they looked out over the immense space. The empty red velvet seats and the Tabor Box held their attention for a long time.

I stood aside, observing their apparent fascination of the interior of this great place.

Presently, the men's conversation came to an abrupt end, and I was intensely aware of the great silence that suddenly came over the building. The men continued to stand motionless, centerstage, surveying the entire area over and over again. The stillness was eerie. If ever there were ghosts of the past in the Tabor Opera House, I could believe that they were there at that moment!

I felt a little uneasy from this long silence. There was a strangeness about the "spell" that seemed to have captured both men. Undoubtedly, they had stepped back into memory, reliving the entire incredible Tabor story.

Suddenly, the silence was broken by a loud voice. "I've got it, I've got it!" exclaimed one of the men.

Back to reality now, they both walked across the stage several more times before they told me that they felt they had just received the inspiration they came for, and they gratefully thanked me, shook my hand and departed—never to be seen by me again. I didn't know it then, but I had just witnessed the birth of that esteemed theater production, "The Ballad of Baby Doe" whose world premiere was held at the Central City Opera House in 1956!

Actor Edward G. Robinson, who starred in the 1933 movie "Silver Dollar," a story about the Tabors. His inscription (upper right) reads: "To Mrs. E. Furman. Silver Dollar was one of the most enjoyable films I ever appeared in. Warm regards, Edward G. Robinson."

Tabor Opera House, Leadville. From The Denver Public Library Western Collection.

DENVER-LEADVILLE STAGE

This photo shows a painting of *The Denver-Leadville Coach. Hanging on the plaster walls of The Windsor Hotel, Denver, Colorado, the original painting was nearly life-size. Note the wall lathing at bottom of picture. The Windsor was being razed in 1960 when this picture was taken. The following day, this wall was torn down, and the painting crumbled with the rest of the debris. Photo from The Tabor Opera House Display, Leadville. Courtesy of J.P. Lester, Jr.*

H.A.W. Tabor. Photo courtesy of The Denver Public Library Western Collection.

Augusta Tabor. Photo from T Denver Public Library Weste Collection.

N. Maxcy Tabor, son of Augu and H.A.W. Tabor.
Photo courtesy of The Denver Public Library Western Collection.

Hence, the Tabor name is perpetuated by this same grand opera, helping the Tabor imprint to live on, in the pages of history.

CONSTRUCTION

TABOR—that magical name—continues to echo 'round the world! Few are here today who haven't heard of the early-day mining bonanza king, Horace A.W. Tabor. The story of the fabulous fortune he made so quickly and lost almost as rapidly, is well-renowned as one of Colorado's most colorful pioneer sagas.

It was after experiencing this sudden rise to the glittering pinnacle of wealth that Tabor decided to erect the Tabor Opera House in Leadville, where it still stands today, a befitting memorial to its illustrious builder.

This world-famous building was constructed on Harrison Avenue, Leadville's main street. Facing westward towards Mounts Massive and Elbert, the stately structure seems to join these peaks as constant sentinels, guarding Leadville's alluring history.

Old newspaper files reveal that J. Thomas Roberts, builder, contracted for $30,000 to erect this new building. Three weeks before the Opera House's completion, J. Thomas Roberts sold his business interest and L.E. Roberts finished the construction. The building's cost, estimated at $78,000, was more than anticipated, an amount which did not include the price of furnishings, scenery and other equipment.

Anxious for the legitimate theater's completion, Leadvillites daily watched the construction in progress. There was a great need for a building such as this. It served as a safety valve for the mass of all classes of people then in Leadville. Prior to this, there were only the saloons. The citizens were justly proud of the beautiful addition to their new city; and they expressed their gratitude to Mr. Tabor for furnishing them with this opera house, so sacred to the legitimate drama.

H.A.W. Tabor had good reason to be proud of this, his first great accomplishment! After all, newspapers of the day acclaimed it ''the largest and best west of the Mississippi.'' The edifice truly was one of the most costly and substantially-built structures in Colorado. At last, there was a first-class amusement place in Leadville where respectable people could go.

The Tabor Opera House was completed in just 100 days from the date of ground-breaking, a record time, considering that Horace Tabor ordered all building materials brought up by wagons that couldn't be purchased in Leadville. No railroad had yet come to Leadville, but reached as far as Webster, at the foot of Kenosha Hill. But there were four lines of Concord stagecoaches running between the trains and Leadville; and still another line of coaches between Canon City and Leadville.

Before the railroad's existence, the circuit actors and actresses traveled to Leadville via these stagecoaches. (Author's Note: I found an old letter behind a desk drawer stating that, on one trip, the stagecoach turned over six times, enroute to Leadville from Denver.)

51

OPENING NIGHT

The Tabor Opera House's grand opening was on the evening of November 20 1879—amidst a flourishing Leadville. The first show was "The Serious Family, a Jack S. Langrishe production, followed by "Who's Who," a comedy.

Besides being Colorado's favorite comedian, Jack S. Langrishe, an Irishman wrote plays and painted scenery. He presented a chaste and superior class amusement. Formerly employed on the New York Tribune, he came west abou 1860, after hearing of the rich gold discoveries. Later, Langrishe went to War ner, Idaho, where he published a local newspaper until his death about the turn the century. His real name was unknown; Langrishe was only an assumed nam

Robert Ball, a one-time Opera House employee, had in his possession a copy the original Opening Night program. This program is now owned by Oliv Reichle, who kindly allowed this writer to reprint the copy contained herein.

Opening night coincided with the lynching of two notorious outlaws b vigilantes. This gruesome incident, occurring the previous evening, took place a partially-completed new building near the Tabor Opera House. Here, the tw outlaws, Frodsham and Stewart, came to a swift end as they were hung by rop from the rafters of the building in progress.

Hushed and uneasy, Leadvillites thronged the streets as soon as they hear about the lynching. This horrible incident put a definite restraint on the Oper House's opening night. Theater-goers were in no mood for frivolity. It is said tha attendance was poor that first night for this reason. Nevertheless, on the followir nights, there was always a packed house.

THE OPERA HOUSE AND A BOOMING LEADVILLE

1879 was the year of the great boom for Leadville. Exciting times were in sto for this mining camp, high in the Rockies!

People of all professions were arriving by the thousands, daily. Not only we the miners settling here with their families, but prominent businessmen we bringing their families to their newly-built Leadville homes, too. The moneye men from the East were investing their capital to develop the rich mines in th area which the prospectors had discovered. What an air of excitement prevailed the sound of the hammer rang through the hills, day and night.

Leadville became so rapidly populated in 1879 that the streets were extreme crowded. Towards the evenings, the multitudes of miners returning from the hil to town caused a giant traffic slow-down. It was almost impossible for anyone advance up the streets, because of the steady flow downward.

On the main streets, those in a hurry chose the middle of the road rather tha the walks. Even there, one took his chances of being run down by the dashir horsemen; or perhaps stagecoaches might come whirling around the corner at an hour.

With the hustle and bustle of settlement in new homes, and establishment new businesses, Leadville was definitely taking on a new look. Harrison Avenu was growing by leaps and bounds. The sagebrush was being cleared away, an

THE PROMPTER.

Volume 1.   LEADVILLE, COLORADO, NOVEMBER 20, 1879.   Number 1.

Programme

Tabor Opera House

Grand Opening!!

The public are respectfully informed that the elegant Temple of Amusement will be opened on THURSDAY, November 20, 1879, introducing, for the first time in Leadville, Colorado's own Comedian

Mr. J. S. LANGRISHE

—AND HIS—

New Star Company

THE VERY BEST COMBINATION WEST OF NEW YORK.

Thursday Evening, November 20,

Will be presented the great Comedy of

Serious Family!

AMINIDAB SLEEK,	. . . .	MR. J. S. LANGRISHE
Captain Murphy Maguire		Mr. E. F. Knowles
Charles Torrens		Mr. C. Norris
Frank Vincent		Mr. J. Duignan
Danvers		Mr. Nalod
Mrs. Ormsly Delmaine		Miss Phoza McAllister
Mrs. Charles Torrens		Miss Clara Rainford
Lady Sowerly Creamly		Miss Sarah Goodrich
Emma Torrens		Miss Julia Parker

To conclude with the laughable Farce of

Who's Who?

MR. SKEPTIC,	. . . . .	MR. J. S. LANGRISHE
Tom Harwood		Mr. W. J. Gross
Frank Oakley		Mr. J. Duignan
George		Mr. Nalod
Mrs. Skepic		Mrs. Julia Parker
Helen Harwood		Miss Clara Rainford

One Price **Clothing** House!
One Price **Clothing** House!

Furnisher, 44 Harrison Avenue.

Opening night program of "The Serious Family," a three-act comedy by Morris Barnett. This play was first performed October 30, 1849 at The Theatre Royal, Haymarket, London, England.

53

Tabor Opera House and Clarendon Hotel, Leadville. Photo courtesy of Mrs. Theresa O'Brien.

Howard Chapin, Pioneer Manager at Leadville's Clarendon Hotel.

J. Sands.

Jacob Sands, friend of Baby Doe Tabor, and owner of Sands Pelton and Company, Menswear. His store once occupied the north section on the ground floor of The Tabor Opera House.

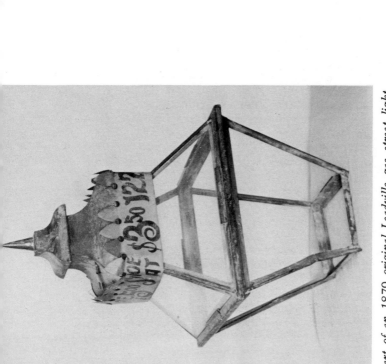

Part of an 1879 original Leadville gas street light. Street lights usually bore advertising. This light came from a street in east Leadville, and was in front of The Crown Shoe Co.

55

people were making improvements on their lots. At that time, only one house stood on the east side of Harrison Avenue, and two or three on the west side. Chestnut Street had been the main street, but now, two blocks north, building on Harrison was progressing beyond that of Chestnut.

Next door to the Opera House, Horace Tabor and W.H. Bush started a new trend on Harrison Avenue in building (away from Chestnut Street) the Clarendon Hotel, ''the Waldorf Astoria'' of its day. Constructed during the winter by contractor J. Thomas Roberts, the plush hotel opened April 10, 1879.

Some predicted failure for an enterprise so far from Chestnut Street. But with these two prominent buildings on Harrison Avenue, the Opera House and the Hotel, others followed, proving the wisdom of Tabor and Bush in selecting this new location.

The massive three-story Tabor Opera House was constructed of stone, brick and iron, and trimmed with Portland cement. The solid brick walls are sixteen inches thick. The frontage measures 60 feet; the length extends 120 feet; and the height reaches 60 feet.

The main entrance is 12 feet wide. Swinging doors offered entry to the spacious corridor and on up a wide flight of stairs, an expanse sufficient to admit a regiment of soldiers.

The ground floor was divided into two spacious store sections, each measuring 23 x 82 feet. A ten-foot stairway leading to the second floor separated the two sections.

The north section was occupied by Sands Pelton and Company, a men's clothing store, the first in Leadville to use solid glass windows. The other section was used as a drug store by J.S. Miller. In the rear was Phil Golding's Saloon, later known as the Cabinet Saloon.

Ultimately behind these businesses was a large wareroom used as a commissary department by the Clarendon Hotel. Connected with this was a private office for W.H. Bush, serving both the Tabor and the Clarendon.

On the front section of the second floor was a luxurious five-room suite, the private quarters of Horace Tabor and W.H. Bush, his Man Friday. Furnished with the latest and most lavish furniture, these suite-rooms also afforded the two men office space. (Even after the Tabors moved to Denver, the private suite was their Leadville home.)

The Tabor Suite is separated from the ornate and elaborate audience room by a five-foot hallway. Six-foot-wide double doorways, in the center, lead to the audience room. On either side of these, two three-foot-wide single doors also lead to the audience room.

The auditorium is 57 feet wide and 65 feet deep. Backstage measures 34 feet in depth, and extends the width of the audience room; and the distance from the floor to the ceiling is 23 feet. The backstage floor, in its entire length, inclines towards the front stage two feet.

The theater has a parquet and dress circle, whose entrance is reached by a second flight of stairs. Seating 400, the dress circle extends, horseshoe-shaped, around the room; and about 450 persons can be comfortably seated on the main floor.

Horace Tabor purchased the finest opera chairs available at the time: Andrews patent opera chairs with adjustable seats. Of Victorian design, they are ornate cast iron, and upholstered in scarlet plush.

The last patent date exposed beneath each seat is January 11, 1876. All seats are numbered with inset plates near the top of the cast iron frame. In the balcony, these seats can still be seen today; and the original benches remain, also, in the back balcony. But some years ago, the original seats on the main floor were removed, and others installed.

In 1879, there were only a few places in the United States to have this type of Andrews seating, and Leadville was one. The usual seating in the other theaters of that day was simple wooden chairs void of padding. These did not suit Mr. Tabor. He wanted only the best for his Tabor Opera House! (The same style elegant seats were used in Booth's, Wallack's and Union Square Theaters in New York; and in the Walnut Street Theater in Philadelphia.)

The total seating capacity of the Tabor Opera House was reported to be 880. But after the Elks' Lodge purchased it at the turn of the century, the seating capacity was increased to 1,000. Theater-goers have said "there just isn't a bad seat in the house," as the view is excellent from every angle.

White and gold hand-turned balusters formed the balustrades around the aforementioned horseshoe circle. The railing was covered with scarlet plush or velvet to correspond with the upholstery on the main floor. Back of the balusters was a lining of sky-blue material.

On either side of the stage are two large proscenium boxes, richly carpeted, mirrored, and upholstered to correspond with the base of the dress circle. Lambrequins and lace curtains added to the beauty of the theater, and gave a bit of privacy to those occupying the boxes. These imported handmade curtains were the most expensive Mr. Tabor could find.

The theater aisles, beautifully carpeted in red, were broom-swept in those days. The walls were painted in brilliant colors. The ceilings were handsomely frescoed. Mid-center of the ceiling, near the stage, was a painting of cherubs, flowers and ribbons, all charmingly done.

The color scheme used in the Tabor Opera House was red, gold, white, and sky-blue, with the blending beauty of everything fully revealed by 72 jets of brightly-burning gas lights.

Stepping inside, it was quite a dazzling sight for one to behold—this brilliantly-illuminated auditorium where everything was new and eye-catching. What a night for those theater-goers to remember on that November 20 in 1879—when the Tabor Opera House opened in a burst of brilliancy!

By November 18, 1879, the Leadville Gas Company was ready for business, and the first gas jets in Leadville's history illuminated the Opera House. Horace Tabor built the gas plant, and the coal used to manufacture the gas was brought to Leadville from Canon City by wagons at a cost of $50 per ton. Soon, Leadville had 90 street lamps, and over 300 dwellings were supplied with gas.

In the Tabor Museum today, a few of these original gas street lights are displayed; and the old gas line still runs through the Opera House. One fixture in the attic remains, too, in its original place. The Opera House's former large chandeliers and fancy glass spiral opaline shades were found stored in the building, and have now been put to use with electricity.

Scene from "Dream City" production on April 13, 1908. Photo courtesy of Olivia Reichle.

Stage of The Tabor Opera House, Leadville, Colorado. Scenery hand-painted on canvas. Taken 1971. Photo courtesy of Glenn Gebhardt, Denver.

An elderly man on a current tour through the Opera House, stated to the author of this book that, in the old days, his father was in charge of dimming the gas lights during the stage productions. The man said that his father, stationed backstage, would sometimes in error dim the footlights too much, and they would immediately be snuffed out.

He went on to say: "I was just a young boy, then. And my job, in helping my father, was to go out onstage and light those footlights, one by one, with a lighted torch."

"What was so bad about that?" I asked.

He replied, "It was the most embarrassing moment of my life. My friends were out there in the audience, and they'd always stomp their feet, and hoot and holler the minute I appeared onstage!"

The Tabor Opera House was furnace-heated and perfectly ventilated. Tabor ordered the furnace to be installed and operating in time for Opening Night, which was quite a feat in itself—having a furnace in Leadville in 1879!

Excellent fire extinguishing arrangements existed. The old extinguishers and hoses can still be seen in the Opera House, with the hoses neatly coiled in place on the ornate cast iron racks attached to the walls. The old patent dates on these are visible, yet, too.

A fifteen-piece orchestra was seated in a circular box on a level with the parquet. Many of the old red and gold band uniforms were left in the dressing rooms.

Tabor's Leadville Opera House was the most perfect place of amusement between Chicago and San Francisco. No wonder people came here from almost everywhere to enjoy the entertainment.

In those days, this stage could accommodate any classical arts production. Measuring 35 by 58 feet, it was a whole hall within itself and flawless in its various arrangements. Rated one of the largest west of New York, the upstage inclined six inches. Around the stage apron were thirty gas jet footlights (mentioned previously.)

SCENERY

There were ten sets of very valuable scenery, all hand-painted on canvas. Due to Leadville's high, dry climate, the stage backdrops and scenery are well-preserved.

The drop curtain was a picturesque masterpiece from the brush of J.B. Lamphere, one of the most talented scenic artists in the West. After working in New York and Philadelphia, Lamphere came to the Opera House promising stage effects as realistic as possible. Representing a glorious mountain scene, the drop curtain featured a charming old castle with a stream running at the base. Following alongside the stream, a rough road ended in a winding canyon. Atop this artistic scene was a life-size portrait of Horace Tabor.

Another curtain, one of the original drops, represented a spectacular view of the Royal Gorge, and cost $1,000. Then there was the forest scene, with its foliage so natural in appearance. As the audience viewed this, they could not detect the thin netting holding the leaves in place. The wooden wings, consisting of three sections for each side of the stage, were often used with the backdrop of a leafy vista ending in a mountain waterfall.

The formal garden scene was lovely to see, and was used with Metropolitan Opera Company productions. The Palace Arch scene, named by the painter, was striking. Another outstanding scene was a series of flats of marble columns and attractive red velvet draperies.

The Plain Chamber scene with a balcony was used for "Romeo and Juliet," and other Shakespearean plays. Then there was the New England kitchen scene, with an alcove. Painted on the reverse side of the Baronial Hall scene, the Prison scene depicted cold and dismal-looking greystone walls.

The Leadville Street scene depicted Harrison Avenue as it looked on the evening of July 4, 1881. This curtain revealed the street with a close-up view of its red brick buildings and gas street lamps. In the hazy distance, afar, was a shadowy grey-blue skyline image near the clouds, which the artist said was Leadville's future skyline 100 years hence.

The largest set of all, encompassing nearly the entire stage, was called "Light Fancy." Its paneled walls were a delicate green, shading to darker green tones near the base, with every flat adorned with rose garlands. This was the favorite set used for High School Commencement Exercises and various other performances held at the Tabor. (Commencement Exercises were conducted here until 1960, when the new Leadville schools were built to accommodate their own stage functions.)

Backstage, there are a few pieces of the original scenery left. They are shorter, and were used before the present stage was enlarged by the Elks' Lodge. And the original curtain was said to have been taken to the Denver Tabor Grand Opera House for use during the 1933 world premiere of the movie "Silver Dollar."

The third floor of the Tabor Opera House contained offices and 25 sleeping rooms for use by the adjoining Clarendon Hotel. These rooms were often occupied by the early-day theater people. A catwalk was constructed from the Clarendon Hotel to the third floor of the Tabor Opera House, as a useful convenience for actors and guests, alike, during inclement weather.

To the third-floor rear of the Opera House was a storeroom 40 by 60 feet for the use of both the Tabor and the Clarendon. This storeroom can still be seen today, with many antique items of interest stored there. In addition, more of the old scenery can be observed on this floor.

During the first winter of the Opera House's existence, several changes were made. A rear window was installed for added ventilation. And in the spring, the auditorium floor was rebuilt on a graduated elevation, improving the view of the stage even more.

ONSTAGE!

The Tabor Opera House was sometimes the site of famous funerals, the first one being that of Charles A.S. Vivian.

Arriving in Leadville in 1879 with Jack Langrishe and Company, Vivian appeared at the Tabor Opera House and other Leadville theaters. A favorite on the variety stage with his dancing and singing, Vivian toured the country with many diverse troupes.

Funeral procession on West 8th Street, Leadville. Notice that the bearse was black, denoting an older person's funeral. White bearses were used, at that time, for young persons. This view, looking East, shows the Presbyterian Church spire in the distance. Photo courtesy of Olivia Reichle.

Born in England, Charles Algernon Sidney Vivian came to America and founded the "Jolly Corks" in 1868. This organization was similar to the "Buffaloes," a social order in his native England, to which he belonged. Later, the Jolly Corks changed their name to "Elks," a name said to have been inspired by an elk's head the members had observed in the room where they were meeting. Since then, the organization has been called the "Benevolent Protective Order of Elks."

Mr. Vivian once lived in 110 East Second Street, Leadville, occupying a small upper front room in the two-story building. The structure was once a boarding house in the former vaudeville theater district.

Vivian died on March 20, 1880 in that little front room. Last rites escorted his body from the funeral parlor to the Tabor Opera House stage, where it laid in state. Then twenty men on horseback preceded a long procession of carriages to Evergreen Cemetery. A band followed, playing "The Dead March from Saul." Returning to Harrison Avenue, they played "Ten Thousand Miles Away," Vivian's favorite song. He had sung this same tune to thousands when he appeared before the footlights. Mr. Vivian's body remained in Evergreen Cemetary until 1889, when it was removed to the Elks' plot of the Boston Lodge.

(Author's Note: When I came to Leadville in 1933, numerous homes and business buildings were standing vacant, their windows boarded up. At that time, the aforementioned old home once occupied by Charles Vivian was vacant, too, with its windows boarded over. Like the surrounding buildings, it became so dilapidated that it was razed in 1934.

The Elks had acquired this building from the city, intending to make the historic spot into a shrine. But they changed their plans, later, thinking it was not worth saving. Had it only been preserved, this could have been a beloved spot to all Elks and to the public. But, as it was, another Leadville landmark was gone forever.)

Another famous funeral held on the Opera House stage was that of John B. (Texas Jack) Omohundro, who died June 28, 1880. An Indian fighter and frontier scout, Texas Jack was a bosom friend and fellow showman of Buffalo Bill Cody.

Mademoiselle Moracchi, an Italian-born world-famous Metropolitan Opera Star and ballet dancer, came to Leadville for an appearance at the Tabor Opera House. Her real name was Guiseppina (Josephine) Moracchi. Eventually, she joined the western show with Texas Jack and Buffalo Bill, where she fell in love with and married the handsome Texas Jack.

While living in Leadville, Texas Jack enlisted in the Tabor Light Cavalry and took part in various functions around the city before his death.

Leadville has perhaps never since witnessed such touching funeral services as those given to Texas Jack's memory. He is buried in Evergreen Cemetary. Buffalo Bill had a monument erected on Texas Jack's grave in 1908 when he came to Leadville again, bringing his Wild West show for a performance.

(In 1965, a female relative of Texas Jack's visited the Tabor Opera House. She was very impressed by his noted history in Leadville. But especially was she sentimental when she walked onstage and sat down for a silent moment in the very setting of Texas Jack's funeral.)

Circuses even performed on the stage of the Tabor Opera House! One circus came to Leadville, and due to the cold weather, refused to unload the animals unless they could perform indoors. Since the Tabor Opera House was the only logical place, it was here that the circus was held.

The circus' management was forced to adjust to an inside performance, but things went smoothly, nonetheless. However, one lady recalled how her mother sat in the fourth row, profoundly apprehensive at being so close to the lions sitting on their haunches near the front of the stage! Amazingly, other Leadvillites remember elephant acts onstage—proof that the floor is solid, indeed!

In those affluent days of 1879 and 1880, it was an unbelievable sight to see audiences shower gold and silver coins upon the Opera House stage. For many a handful of coins was hurled across the gas footlights to some popular star!

One evening, H.A.W. Tabor and W.H. Bush were seated in the private Tabor Box when Gladys Robeson, a popular variety actress of the day, appeared in "red tights that set off her admirable figure." Now, these two gentlemen were friends in business and politics, but were rivals for the attention of every female star playing at the Tabor.

Mr. Tabor tossed a handful of silver dollars across the footlights to this beauty. Mr. Bush, not to be outdone, tossed two handsful. Tabor rose to his feet, and threw four handsful. Finally, their silver was gone, so they ordered more money sent up from the gambling rooms, downstairs.

This time, the two men threw bagsful of gold pieces! As the "battle" raged on, the audience was dazzled by the noisy excitement. And soon, they too joined in, throwing coins onstage until almost every coin in the house was there.

Overwhelmed by this attention, the actress gathered up $5,000 and slipped out the stage door. Her disappearance was a disappointment to both Mr. Tabor and Mr. Bush. For they were hoping for an introduction to her.

The stagehands gathered up even more money backstage after the actress had gone. There are still descendents of those stagehands, living today, who remember the story. Never before nor since has so much money been thrown on the stage. It was listed in history as the $5,000 Story!

In the 1880s, the appearance at the Tabor by Oscar Wilde, British lecturer, poet and critic, caused a flurry of excitement throughout the mining town. Moreover, his style of dress aroused feverish curiousity among the citizens. Even his lecture entitled "The Practical Application of the Aesthetic Theory to Exterior and Interior House Decoration, with Observations on Dress and Personal Ornament" was cause for wonder!

For the dramatic occasion, the stage was set with a balcony scene, and decorated with bric-a-brac. Wilde stepped out on the stage dressed in an elegant black velvet suit with knee breeches, and black stockings. A Byron collar with a white flossy handkerchief adorned his neck; and a cluster of diamonds glittered from his white shirt-front.

The miners were astonished by the Englishman's mode of dress. What's more, Wilde spoke in a monotone, and they understood very little of what he said. However, later, they decided they liked him because he held his liquor so well. (Before leaving Leadville, the miners took Oscar Wilde down into the Matchless Mine in an ore bucket. Here, deep in the earth, they held a banquet. Wilde

Leadville under martial law, 1880. State troops arrive to help settle mine strike.

Original invitation to Grand Banquet for Ulysses S. Grant, July 24, 1880.

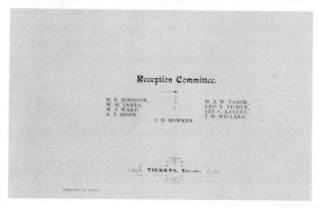

Page 2 of original Grand Banquet Invitation for Ulysses S. Grant.

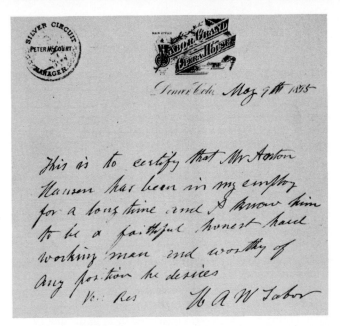

Letter of recommendation written by H.A.W. Tabor May 9, 1895. Photo courtesy of Dr. Nolie Mumey.

Stock certificate dated October 12, 1883 bearing H.A.W. Tabor's signature. Photo courtesy of Mrs. Theresa O'Brien.

related: "The first course was whiskey, the second was whiskey, and the third whiskey!")

Occasionally, the Opera House was used for church services. In addition, many Leadvillites remember the John L. Sullivan and James Corbett boxing matches. Used in these fights, the boxing-ring rope can still be seen, on a tour; and one may also view the old trap door, centerstage, for which there was a variety of uses! After the days of the stage shows came the moving pictures—first the silents and then the talkies. But now the movies are gone and we are back to stage shows again.

TROUBLES AND CELEBRATIONS

In 1880, the year of the great mine strike, troubled times came to Leadville. And whatever happened in Leadville, of course, had its effects on the Tabor Opera House. Miners and smelter workers wanted higher wages, and the strike brought disaster. Mine owners held a meeting behind locked doors of the Tabor Opera House, and drew up a series of resolutions concerning the strike.

On June 14, the Opera House was closed down, as the strike situation got out of hand. Vigilantes and militia failed to settle the circumstances, and martial law was declared in Leadville. Troops were quartered there until June 17, when most of the trouble ceased and the strike collapsed.

When at last the troops succeeded to maintain law and order, the Opera House reopened with the production, "Enoch Arden," and the town was once more back to normal.

After July 22, 1880, when the Denver and Rio Grande Western Railroad arrived in Leadville, travel was much easier, and the town didn't seem so isolated from the world. That specific July day was a significant one for Leadville, marking one of its momentous social events. General Ulysses S. Grant was the official guest for this carefully-planned occasion.

General Grant and his party arrived in the evening. The general was honored by a thirteen-gun salute and welcomed by 5,000 people. A hundred-voice choir furnished the singing; and a parade representing Leadville society favorably impressed the General and his party, (consisting of Mr. and Mrs. Tabor, The Colonel Mrs. Fred Grant, Mr. W. Smith, cousin of Mrs. Fred Grant, and Doctor and Mrs. Bell.) The visitors were astonished by the vast progress made in Leadville, and the joyous celebration of the completed railroad will never be forgotten.

Later that same evening, the Knowles Troupe presented "Our Boarding House," in the handsomely decorated Opera House interior. A full house was present, as Leadville's most notable people attended, hoping to see the celebrated guests.

When General Grant entered the auditorium, the crowd emitted enthusiastic cheers. Then escorts accompanied the Grant party to the Tabor Box, while the orchestra played "Hail to the Chief."

After the performance, the party proceeded in carriages to City Hall for the grand reception and ball, a most elaborate affair. After the introductions, the dancing commenced with the General, himself, leading "Veteran's Quadrille."

General Grant and his party enjoyed the Leadville visit so much that they stayed on another five days. During this, a benefit was held for the Richie Light Guards, a police organization; and "Ours" by T.W. Robertson was the production. General Grant and Governor J.L. Routt were present, with both gentlemen showing their obvious approval.

The extended visit provided an opportunity for the Grant party to visit the mining area. They enjoyed a trip over Fryer Hill before attending a Grand Banquet, held at the Clarendon Hotel to honor General U.S. Grant. (An original invitation to this Grand Banquet can be seen today in the Tabor Opera House Museum.)

On another occasion, Tabor, as Lieutenant Governor, and his first wife, Augusta, returned to Leadville to attend the Republican Nominating Convention. Met by the cavalry at the train, Tabor and Augusta were welcomed home by a crowd of people plainly showing their respect for Tabor and their love for Augusta. The Tabor Light Guard Ball followed, at City Hall, where the conservative Mrs. Tabor was attired in an elegant black silk dress, trimmed with white lace, and even sported radiant diamond jewelry.

(Divorcing her husband later, Augusta Tabor moved from Leadville in 1880, and seldom returned. In 1883, Tabor married Elizabeth "Baby Doe" McCourt in Washington, D.C.)

Another time, in 1884, Tabor, as ex-U.S. Senator, came to Leadville via the South Park train, and was met at the depot by the National Guard, headed by the First Brigade Band. Most of Leadville's citizens again were there to meet him, coming both in carriages and afoot. After the congratulations, a procession formed to escort the ex-Senator to his elaborate suite in the Tabor Opera House.

That evening, soldiers presented "The Union Spy" to an immense Opera House audience. When Tabor, arrayed in his regimental uniform, entered the auditorium, the people gave him a standing ovation and loudly cheered him as he made his way to the Tabor Box. Afterwards, Tabor was escorted to the Armory for a banquet, where numerous speeches were given, eulogizing the ex-Senator's services to Leadville. Horace Tabor responded with a speech, expressing his appreciation for the hearty and unexpected celebration his comrades had prepared for him. The banquet was a rousing triumph, and Tabor's hand was shaken by thousands, irrespective of political party affiliation.

The Tabor Opera House reached the peak of its renown in 1880 through 1882, continuing in its usual style with good companies and good audiences. The Tabor stage was trodden by each actor and actress ever to attain distinction, in those days.

Successful plays from Wallack's, Daly's, the Madison Square's, or Union Square's Theaters of New York toured the nation, and Leadville was a regular stop-over for the booking circuits. Clearly, the Tabor Opera House had the best performers of the New York stage.

Mr. Tabor loved the theater, and made certain that culture was brought to this rugged mining camp. Leadville audiences expected the best, and Mr. Tabor never accepted a substitute for any performer, either.

(By 1880, six variety theaters thrived in Leadville, but a decline followed, and only two survived. Shorter seasons were evident in the legitimate theater, but the

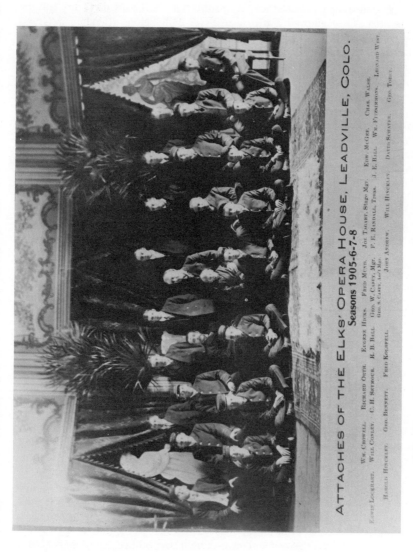

ATTACHES OF THE ELKS' OPERA HOUSE, LEADVILLE, COLO.
Seasons 1905-6-7-8

WM. CROWELL.   RICHARD ORTH.   EUGENE HOSS.   FRED MUND.   JOE TIGERT, STAGE MGR.   EDW. MOYER.   CHAS. WALSH.
WILL CONLEY.   C. H. SEYMOUR.   R. B. BALL.   GEO. W. CAREY, MGR.   F. E. RANDALL, TREAS.   J. E. BALL.   WM. FITZSIMMONS.   LEONARD WEST.
EDWIN LOCKHART.   GEO. BECKETT.   FRED KOLMPEL.   GEO. S. CAREY, ASS'T MGR.   JOHN ANDREW.   WILL HINCKLEY.   DAVID SCHAYER.   GEO. TOBIN.
HAROLD HINCKLEY.

Elks Opera House stagehands. Photo courtesy of Mrs. Olivia Reichle.

68

Program (page 1) of 1888 Graduation Exercises held onstage at The Tabor Opera House.

Program (page 2) of 1888 graduation exercises. Notice only three young students graduated!

Keep the Watch Wound.

CLASS OF '88.

Evangeline Alberta Alfred

Rosa Lillie Beitzmann

Hattie Zimmer Yost

ORDER OF EXERCISES.

TRIO,	*From Barber of Seville.*	Rossini.
	MISSES O'BRIEN, WILLIAMSON AND BEEDE.	
INVOCATION,	REV. L. L. KNEELAND.	
SERENADE,	TEMPLE (MALE) QUARTETTE.	
SALUTATORY,	MISS ALFRED.	
PIANO SOLO,	MRS. L. M. GODDARD.	
ORATION, "Life Through a Prism,"	MISS YOUNG.	
VOCAL SOLO,	"*Margarite,*"	MRS. E. A. GUILBAULT.
ESSAY, "The Future of Colorado,"	MISS BEITZMANN.	
CORNET DUET,	ORCHESTRA ACCOMPANIMENT.	
ESSAY, "Are the Planets Inhabited?"	MISS ALFRED.	
VOCAL SOLO,	MRS. F. SCHNEIDER.	
VALEDICTORY,	MISS YOUNG.	
CLARIONET SOLO,	ORCHESTRA ACCOMPANIMENT.	
PRESENTATION OF DIPLOMAS,	THE PRESIDENT OF THE BOARD.	
OVERTURE,	LEADVILLE QUINTETTE.	
BENEDICTION,	REV. H. C. ARMSTRONG.	

BOARD OF EDUCATION:

MAX BOEHMER President

L. WORCESTER Secretary

C. A. SEYMOUR   JOHN HARVEY

Superintendent, W. W. WATTERS.

ell-known actors of the day still came to town. With the decline, the week's
rformances were cut to three nights, then two nights and finally the town
came a one-night stand on the "Silver Circuit" between Denver and Salt Lake
ty.)

CHANGES IN OWNERSHIP

During the financial panic of 1893, Mr. Tabor, as well as many others, lost
verything. Now, having changed owners, the Opera House was known as The
Veston. Drawn West by the 1859 Pike's Peak gold rush excitement, Mr. Weston
nd family had arrived in California Gulch July 14, 1860. Engaged in mining and
anching near Leadville, Weston was also a State Senator; practiced law; and held
leading position in the California Gulch I.O.O.F. Lodge.

The Weston family now occupied the Tabor Suite, but continued to operate the
pera House with little change. Famous actors of the era still made one-night
ppearances. Between the elaborate productions, minstrel shows and second-rate
oupes filled in. Thus, as the leading center for all Leadville events, the Weston
ontinued in the Tabor tradition, with noted actors of the time appearing such as
ffie Coghlan, Edward Harrington, Frederic Warde, and John Philip Sousa's
and.

The Nineties were hard years in Leadville. Yet, during those difficult times, the
Veston saved itself by booking the best entertainment on one night, and then
taying dark the other six nights of the week. Political meetings were also con-
ucted at the Opera House; and in 1897, "Wonderful Magniscope" appeared,
hich made scenes move and people in the picture appeared alive.

Mr. Weston died in 1897, and Mrs. Weston took over the management.
Jewspapers boasted of her as being one of only three existing women managers of
pera houses in the country.

During the latter part of the century, the Weston held excellent shows such as
ur days of grand opera productions by the Metropolitan Opera Company; and
he appearances by such renowned actors and actresses as Helen Modjeska,
.athryn Kidder, and Louise James.

1901 marked another change in the Tabor Opera House's ownership. Due to
nancial difficulties, Mrs. Weston sold out to Doctor J.H. Herron, who in turn,
mmediately sold out to the Elks' Lodge for $12,000.

Closing the theater for six months, the Elks remodeled and repaired the
uilding. Spending $25,000, they now had both space suitable for lodge rooms
nd for continuing the theater's operation.

With the building known as the Elks' Opera House, managed by George Casey,
he Elks opened December 11, 1902 with the musical comedy "Florodora."

The Elks made large changes in the theater. The original walnut finish was
tered to a light-colored paint. A new stage was added on the back, increasing the
ating capacity to nearly 1,000. (The dressing rooms underneath the stage are
till in use for present-day shows; and full-length walnut-framed mirrors are yet
mong the many furniture items displayed and used in this area.)

Next door, the Clarendon Hotel saloon and lobby continued serving as a club
r the "Carbonate kings." Here, banquets were given to not only Ulysses S.

Grant and wife, but also to General Sherman, the Duke of Cumberland, Commodore Vanderbilt, and Jay Gould, U.S. financier and capitalist. The hotel's celebrated food was prepared by Monsieur L. Lapierce from Delmonico's in New York. The Clarendon served as a hospital during the 1918 flu epidemic; and the famous old landmark was razed in the 1930s.

Having plans for a new building, the Elks' Lodge sold the Opera House to Mrs. Florence A. Hollister on January 12, 1955. Mrs. Hollister, as owner number five, again changed the name of the building—this time restoring the original historical American landmark's name back to "Tabor."

Having lived in Leadville for years prior to the purchase, Mrs. Hollister had grown fond of Leadville history. She was a retired school teacher and artist from Minnesota. And with her deep love of history, she felt the famous old place should be restored and preserved. And with her interest in art, she realized the hand-painted scenery was priceless, and therefore should be protected for everyone to see and enjoy.

Although the purchase of the building and the initial restoration took nearly all of her life's savings, Mrs. Hollister never once regretted her sacrifice, believing this new venture would benefit and bring pleasure to many.

RESTORATION, RENOVATION AND TOURISTS!

In her 70s, Mrs. Hollister chose to spend her retirement years with her daughter, the author of this book. So together, we started this novel business adventure.

In the beginning, no one thought we'd entered a wise investment. But despite the discouraging remarks we received, we kept right on working! Today, the opinions are reversed, and many people think it is a very worthwhile endeavor.

Mrs. Hollister opened the Tabor Opera House's doors to tourists and other interested persons, at once. Though breathless, she climbed the stairs time after time, giving tours alone. She cherished the dear friends she made on these tours, and enjoyed the correspondence resulting from these friendships.

Our first project was to repair the Opera House's entire roof. Next, the stage floor was sanded and a preservative finish applied. Hundreds of nail holes were filled in—holes resulting from the constant procedure of setting up and taking down scenery, through the years.

Enormous sections of plaster were replaced, throughout the building. The ceiling under the balcony was removed and replaced. Additionally, a tremendous amount of labor went into the thorough cleaning of the theater's interior. Due to the extreme height involved, this task required much more time than was anticipated.

Painting the theater's interior was the next project considered, as we wanted to restore the original colors. When we took over, the interior was green. But with the help of a friend, we learned the shades that were once used, and the paint supplier mixed the colors as we directed. A light blue ceiling was completed, and dark red walls soon followed. Some of the cast iron frames of the original Andrews opera chairs have been cleaned, and painted gold, giving the desired effect of the original red-and-gold color scheme.

fth owner of The Tabor Opera House, Mrs. Florence A. Hollister, at age 75.

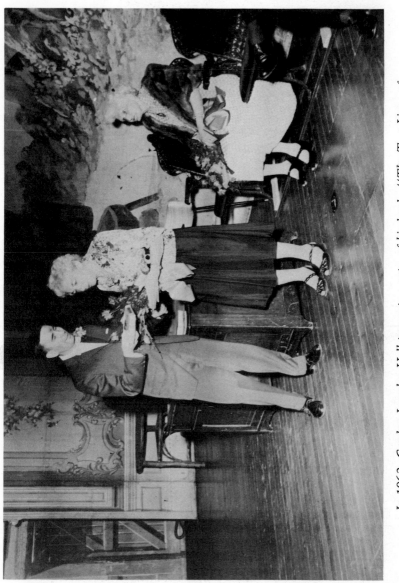

In 1962, Gordon Langley Hall presents a copy of his book, "The Two Lives of Baby Doe," to Florence A. Hollister, owner, onstage at The Tabor Opera House. Seated is Mrs. Theres O'Brien, long-time maid at The Opera House, who had

rs. Theresa O'Brien stands in front of an original bookcase in the second-floor
bor Suite. Rooms were under restoration when this photo was taken in 1965. A
nver Post photo.

is stage view clearly shows the backs of the exquisite Andrews Opera Chairs in
e Parquet. Photo courtesy of Glenn Gebhardt, Denver.

75

Tabor Opera House Box Office. Denver Post photo.

Left, Mrs. Theresa O'Brien giving tour at Tabor Opera House, Leadville, Colo 1971. Right, Mrs. Glenn Gebhardt of Denver, Colorado. Photo by Glen Gebhardt, Denver.

A large painting was taken from the attic and hung on the balcony wall. The opposite side of this wall proved to be the ideal spot for Mr. H.A.W. Tabor's picture, a gift from the Denver Tabor Grand Opera House.

The furnace was repaired; and the plumbing and the electrical work were partially completed. A new embossed metal ceiling was installed in part of the Tabor Suite, and replastering nearly completed. Some repainting of the walls in this area has also been accomplished, and velvet draperies are being made for the large windows.

Soon, the tourists began appearing in larger numbers, and Mrs. Hollister continued to enjoy showing her Opera House to the interested visitors. Then, one day, Mrs. Theresa O'Brien approached Mrs. Hollister, asking if she could help with the tours, and my mother employed her, at once. Not long afterwards, failing health hindered Mrs. Hollister from continuing her tours. So Mrs. O'Brien took complete charge of the tours, and engaged several more aides to help her.

Having once known "Baby Doe" (the second Mrs. Tabor) Mrs. O'Brien is well-suited in her work. She always charms her visitors, daily, with her first-hand accounts of pioneer life in Leadville and with her piquant stories about Baby Doe.

Currently, Mrs. O'Brien continues as head tour guide, loving her work and the Tabor Opera House. The tourists adore her, in return, and come back, year after year, to hear this delightful lady. No person as capable for her job exists as does Mrs. Theresa O'Brien!

Dependable and faithful, her cheerful manner and interesting presentation enchants the tourists. I consider her to be a most pleasing person with whom to be associated. A tour with Mrs. O'Brien is truly a trip into the past. What a treasure of memories she possesses! On a tour with her, it is possible for one to relive again and again those great days of long ago, through Mrs. O'Brien's graphic words.

On February 10, 1965, Mrs. Florence Hollister passed away, at 83 years of age—bringing down the curtain on the life of the dear little lady who had, just ten years before, purchased the Tabor Opera House. Mrs. Hollister, at the age of 73, started this large restoration project rather late in life, exemplifying what one brave woman did, despite her advanced years.

Always, her courageous character qualities led her successfully through life. May her spirit live on in all the others who are continuing her restoration work at the Tabor Opera House! It was Mrs. Hollister's wish that everyone in this generation and in all future generations could enjoy this historical building. For, indeed, this Opera House is not only Leadville's heritage, but the heritage of the world, as well.

Florence Eliza Ayars Livingston Hollister was born in Freeborn County, Minnesota on September 2, 1881. (Incidentally, this was the period when the Tabor Opera House was undergoing its greatest years.) This was the lady destined to save the Opera House from destruction in 1955. Thanks to Mrs. Hollister, we still have a Tabor Opera House!

One of five children, Mrs. Hollister was born to Charles C. and Susan M. Pierce Ayars. Her father was born in New Jersey, and came West with his parents in a covered wagon in 1855. The family experienced the usual pioneering hardships, including those of homesteading.

Mrs. Hollister's ancestors date back to the early history of the United State through one Robert Ayars, who was born in England in 1650, and who came t Newport, Rhode Island in 1664. Other members of the Ayars family came t America from England during the Mayflower days.

Mrs. Hollister, herself, was a North Dakota pioneer, homesteading there as young woman. During her early years as a school teacher, she recalled the ne towns springing up in North Dakota; and experienced many troublesome burder there, along with the other first settlers. Thus, she too, left her mark on the page of Time.

Mrs. Hollister thoroughly relished spending her last years in Leadville con nected with the Tabor Opera House. Among her treasures was an autographe photo of Gordon Langley Hall, journalist, playwright and biographer. He penne the picture as follows: "For Leadville's First Lady—Florence Hollister, 1962. She was touched by this tribute presented to her when Hall came to Leadville t introduce his new book, "The Two Lives of Baby Doe."

When the Tabor Opera House passed into Florence Hollister's ownership, th first appearance was by Rubinoff with his violin, sponsored by the local Lior Club. I, myself, recall Rubinoff, on the stage, commending Mrs. Hollister fc saving the building. "Don't change it," he said. "Just fix it up, and keep it as used to be, as much as possible!"

After the death of Mrs. Hollister, my mother, I have continued on with th management and restoration much the same as she did. I am most anxious t complete the Tabor Suite, where I have restored a number of the original fur niture pieces. Some were in good condition, while others were badly broken, an needing repair and upholstery.

A very generous and kind gentleman, John Seymour, (a descendent of th Twenty-Mule Team Borax Family) has donated additional valuable Victoria furniture for the Suite, contributing large hand-carved bedroom pieces. In ex cellent condition, this beautiful furniture is a welcome addition. Mr. Tabc himself could not have selected anything finer!

The late Fred Reichle once spent considerable time at the Tabor Opera Hous telling this writer of the old days when he was a stagehand here; of how he peddle bill posters in 1905; and that Joe Tagert was stage manager then. Previously, Jc Tagert used to ignite the city's gas street lights. He was a familiar sight in tho days, riding on horseback, and carrying a lighted torch.

Sauntering along with me through the Tabor, Mr. Reichle pointed out th various items he remembered. In the foyer, he gestured to the picture of Charle Hanford and said: "He was a great Shakespearean actor. So was Mr. Hanford wife, Marie Drofnah."

"See," he added, "Drofnah was her stage name, and if you'll notice, it's jus 'Hanford' spelled backwards!"

Mr. Reichle continued: "Charles Hanford could so cleverly inpersonate woman that even his friends couldn't tell the difference."

Continuing to meander, Mr. Reichle stated to me enthusiastically: "There John Philip Sousa! I remember his white gloves. He always wore them, yo know, and he threw them away *after* each performance." Then, as an a

Opera House's front view, as it looked *1965. A Denver Post photo.*

View looking over The Tabor Box to the stage where Mrs. Evelyn E. Furman, present Opera House owner, is seated. A Denver Post photo.

Tabor Opera House stage, with Evelyn Furman, owner, seated thereon. A Denver Post photo.

terthought, Mr. Reichle added: "I wish I'd picked up a pair. They'd be wort quite a sum now!"

Smiling as he thought of these days of yore, Mr. Reichle continued: "On night, Mr. Sousa forgot his white gloves, and I was the one who had to go back his hotel room and get them."

"Goodness! How many pairs did he keep on hand?" I asked.

"Oh, a stack about like that," answered Mr. Reichle, designating with bot hands a pile measuring the space of several dozen pairs.

We proceeded to the stage. By this time, several tourists were following u having overheard our conversation. It isn't often that one hears such things firs hand!

The tourists were so delighted with Fred Reichle that he came to the Oper House a number of times after that, and simply "took over" the tours. I can st picture him, yet, in my memory, standing onstage, and zealously showing th tourists exactly how John Philip Sousa led the band!

One day, Mr. Reichle and I were discussing the ladders on the backstage wal These long ladders lead to the fly where a network of ropes are fastened, to contr the scenery.

"You know, we stagehands used to watch the shows from up there in the fly," he said to me.

Craning my neck upwards at the soaring height, I exclaimed, "My! You had grandstand seat there, didn't you?"

"Oh, yes," he replied. "All except for one show, and that was 'Brewster' Millions.' "

"Why was that?" I queried.

"Well—over the top of the entire stage was a canopy and we couldn't see thing!" (Brewster's Millions is the story of a character who was supposed to ge rid of all his money. But no matter which way he turned, he made more and more instead.)

Then Mr. Reichle mentioned the Westons, recalling when Mrs. Weston wa left to operate the theater. "She fell heir to the mortgage" was his comment "There weren't many shows in those days. The rent she received from the store downstairs was about the only revenue."

"When I was here, this Opera House was a one-night stand," continued Mr Reichle. "There were two circuits out of Denver. One played the Denver Tabor Grand and perhaps the Auditorium or Broadway Theater. After three or fou nights' billing in Denver, either one circuit or the other would always come up here to Leadville," he explained. "These circuits played Salt Lake City and Sar Francisco. Leadville's legitimate theater was associated with the Tabor Grand ir Denver, and the performers and theatrical companies appeared in both cities."

Fred Reichle related the astounding entertainments given by Houdini, the magician, who did everything from pulling rabbits out of hats to the most com plicated magic acts of all time. "Most magicians of the day had a table with a purple velvet cover situated in centerstage. It was located near the uncovered trap door for obvious reasons, and I guess that's how he fooled us!"

"Thank you, Mr. Reichle. I'm grateful for the time you spend here, explaining all this to me. Come back tomorrow," I said.

But tomorrow and the following tomorrows were not to be, for Fred Reichle passed away December 28, 1965. What a charming little man he was, and how I miss him!

Today, touring visitors are taken backstage, where steps from either side lead to the dressing-room area, beneath the stage. A visiting tourist once stated: "These dressing rooms are all as large as ones anywhere in the United States—even New York." At the Tabor, the leading lady's dressing room is on the north, and the leading man's on the south. Much of the old furniture and stage properties still remain here, and are in use.

The stars' dressing rooms were furnished with a couch. Old dressers, etc., repainted years ago, are gradually being restored to their original walnut or mahogany finish. The dressing rooms' original carpeting still covers the floors, though worn threadbare—a reminder of the past's profusion of footsteps and the commotion of preparations before show-time.

As we view these precious theater remnants of the glorious yesteryear, I can almost see actress Anna Held preparing to go onstage. With her make-up job almost finished, she is decked out in a gorgeous dress with a long train. And are those *real* diamonds flashing in the heels of her shoes? Once onstage, Anna Held never failed to mesmerize her idolizing audiences.

One day, a small lady in her 80s came through the Opera House on a guided tour with me. "I used to be a chorus girl on that stage when I was young," she said.

"How did you dress?" I asked.

She replied, "We had knee-length skirts and wore high heels, which was quite daring in those days!"

Continuing, she offered: "I wasn't famous. But Anna Held was the famous one of my day! Anna wasn't in good health, and had to be carried to the Opera House from the hotel. She rested on a couch behind the scenery between acts. Neither the audience nor her fans knew this, because she always managed to put on an exceptional performance, somehow."

"What show stands out in your memory as the greatest?" I asked the elderly woman.

"Ben Hur," she replied, and pointed to the double door backstage, which leads out on St. Louis Avenue. "The stagehands brought six horses and a chariot through there," she said.

"How did they *ever* do Ben Hur here?" I asked, astonished.

"They built a revolving treadmill for the stage floor, making the horses and chariot look like they were going at a tremendous speed! But one night, a wheel flew off the chariot and landed right there!" she said, pointing down to the north side of the orchestra pit.

"Goodness!" I uttered. "Was anyone hurt?"

"No," she answered. "There were about 25 stagehands in those days. And they rescued that wheel in no time, and put it right back into place."

An aged gentleman, living in Denver, once informed me: "I've seen many wonderful shows in that old Opera House when it was known as the Weston. I used to carry in buckets of coal for Mrs. Weston when she lived in the Tabor Suite.

She used to let me in free to see the shows through the second-floor door leading into the balcony.''

"Later on," he added, smiling, "When it was known as the Elks' Opera House, I used to go around in back to the Opera House Barns, and rent the best carriage available. Then I'd bring my girlfriend and we'd see other great shows like 'Florodora.' Usually, we had seats in Row E, center. There were three lines of chorus girls in those days. Their costumes looked very glamorous in the footlights. We also saw 'Uncle Tom's Cabin' . . .'' and the aged gentleman went on to remark to me how real the blocks of ice looked as Little Eva went tripping along, in that latter-mentioned play.

Another day later on, a lady in her 80s joined a tour I was giving. She said to me: "I used to play on this stage when I was young. I was only seven years old at the time, and traveled with my mother, who was a singer."

With a faraway look in her eye, she continued: "I played the part of Little Eva in 'Uncle Tom's Cabin'!''

Immediately, the "Uncle Tom's Cabin" story which I'd heard about from the elderly gentleman previously, flashed through my mind. Here was Little Eva standing in front of me, after all those passing years!

Curious about the blocks of ice which looked so real, I asked her: "What were those blocks of ice made of?"

"They were made of heavy cardboard, and cleverly painted by the best artist available in those days," she explained. Then she asked, "Are the dressing rooms still here?"

"Yes," I answered.

Despite a bad limp, the former Little Eva nonetheless struggled to descend into the dressing rooms via the orchestra entrance steps. There, she pointed out her dressing room to me.

Since I love to talk to interesting people such as she, I hated to see her leave. But, as she was departing the Opera House, she spied an empty wooden chair by the main entrance.

"That empty chair brings back memories. I used to attend Sunday School in those days, and there would always be one empty chair, just like that one, on each side of me. You see, since I was a showgirl, the other children were not allowed to sit by me," she explained.

Then she bade me goodbye. And once again, I felt enlightened by another tidy bit of nostalgic history.

During the theater's early days, scenery and equipment were hauled by many wagonloads to Leadville. After the arrival of the railroads, entire trainloads were brought in. Then large wagons came from the depot, delivering load after load, to the huge double doors at the rear of the Opera House stage. It took hours to unpack the scenery, trunks and equipment.

Brought in was such equipment as a boiler to make volcanoes explode onstage, and other amazing outfits to make the dramas as realistic as possible. At times, the stagehands stayed all night at the Opera House to accomplish the tremendous work involved in setting up the scenery. One stagehand recalls curling up in one of the boxes some nights to catch a few winks of sleep. It took so long to do a perfect job, there wasn't much time for sleep, though!

Another gentleman remembered the great lengths the stagehands went to, in order to obtain the desired effect for the shows. For one production, he explained to me how they covered the stage floor with a heavy canvas, and then painted this canvas to resemble the sea.

"There were such good artists in those days. The waves looked so natural, I just thought I was looking at a real ocean," he said. "On top of this canvas was placed a large ship. And you'll never guess what was under that canvas!"

"What was it?" I asked.

"A whole bunch of people," he stated, "Just a 'bumping their heads up and down, making it look just like the real tossing sea!"

In 1968, I took Cornelia Otis Skinner on a Tabor Opera House tour. (Being an actress herself, she was especially interested in the Tabor.) Nearing the end of the tour, we took the right stairway from the stage to the dressing rooms.

Cornelia Otis Skinner stepped inside the leading man's dressing room at the foot of the stairs. After a moment of silence, she exclaimed "Just think! My father, Otis Skinner, was right here!"

She explained to me, then, how her father had played at the Opera House in the early 1880s, and that he was Helen Modjeska's leading man. Afterward, Cornelia Otis Skinner informed me that since she didn't see her father's picture among the others in the foyer, she would send me one. And as soon as she returned to New York, she promptly sent me a photo of Otis Skinner dressed as Hamlet!

On another tour day through the Tabor, a gentleman, now living in Nebraska, related to me that his father and mother were both connected with the theater. His father was a carpenter and his mother was the wardrobe mistress. "Those stage carpenters could engineer anything—even make it rain, or make volcanoes explode," he said.

I was delighted to then receive an explanation as to exactly how everything was arranged for the magnificent "Ben Hur" production.

On still another day, two ladies made the tour with me, informing how their grandparents lived in Leadville during the great mining boom. The grandfather ran a saloon, and the grandmother was a seamstress who sewed for the performers, never using a pattern, and always providing a perfect fit.

Another day, an older rather plump lady approached me, to take the tour. There was a heavy smell of alcohol on her breath, and she seemed inebriated.

As the tour ended, she said to me, indignantly: "Well! This was a good tour, but you didn't tell me about the white satin chair that Baby Doe sat on!"

Somewhat surprised and taken aback, I said: "*You* tell *me* about that."

"I remember the white satin chair here in this box," she stated, and described it to me. "I used to be in charge of the costumes in the dressing rooms," she added. (Later, I discovered her stories were true. She knew what she was talking about, after all. A noted seamstress of her day, she made hats and bonnets her specialty.)

After our conversation, the intoxicated woman stepped typsily upon the stage, sat down at the piano, and played various melodies beautifully! Her ability amazed me. And years afterward, I learned she had played the piano long ago in a saloon on Second Street.

One never knows what a day at the Tabor brings forth!

LOOKING BACK

As I continue with the restoration and tours of the Tabor Opera House, I ofte recall when I first arrived in Leadville the summer of 1933.

I had just finished one year at Milton College in Wisconsin, and had intended t return to my Minnesota home. Instead, I accepted a summer job in Wisconsi doing a family's housework and caring for their six-year-old girl. Since this wa during the Depression, I felt fortunate to have any kind of work. Jobs were scarce and I badly needed money for my next year of college.

After several weeks, the family for whom I worked asked me if I would like t accompany them to Leadville, Colorado.

Surprised, I replied, "That sounds great!" And after inquiring more about th proposed trip, I became more and more interested in it.

My mother was not in favor of my new venture. But the father of the family ha been Professor of Geology at Dartmouth College. He offered to tutor me i geology without cost, which would enable me to pick up extra college cred during the summer. It was only because of this that my mother finally consente that I could go.

Westward bound by car, the most pleasurable part of the trip to me was betwee Denver and Leadville, because I had never before seen mountains!

The day we arrived in Leadville and stopped at the old Vendome Hotel was one well remember. For it was then and there that the name "Tabor" reached m young ears, and I wanted to know more.

After we registered, and were settled in our new quarters, I ventured down t the hotel lobby. Enroute, I was very impressed with the antique appearance c everything I saw. In the center of the tiled floor was a huge fountain, in which th water cascaded into a large round rustic base below. Here, I saw mountain trou swimming, the first I'd seen.

"Tell me about the Tabors," I pleaded to the lady clerk at the desk.

Though I'd only arrived in Leadville that afternoon, I simply couldn't contai my eagerness over both the Tabors and the town.

"Mr. Tabor was the greatest!" she replied, emphasizing the word "Tabor" i a way that suggested extreme prominence. "He made millions and spent it all, she added, and I was all ears!

"Mr. Tabor died years ago," continued the desk clerk. "But Baby Do sometimes stays in this hotel." Then in a lower tone, she leaned over closer to m and said, "People are curious about her, and like to see her, if they can. Sh dresses in old clothes, and lives up at the Matchless," and she waved a hand i that direction.

My obvious interest prompted the clerk to go on. "Mr. Tabor helped build thi hotel, and it was called the Tabor Grand then." (In 1972, the Vendome Hote was renamed the Tabor Grand Hotel.)

"See—here's Mr. Tabor's signature in this old hotel register," she said pointing to an open book in the glass showcase before me.

The family whom I worked for included me in their various trips around th Leadville area, and I was enthralled by the old mines and ancient log buildings The board walks and unusual fences also caught my attention.

The Professor of Geology (with whom I'd come to Leadville) was a member of a group just starting a placer mining operation in California Gulch. Therefore, I had the opportunity to watch this process, and I was fascinated by the small particles of gold accumulating in the sluice boxes. One day, a geologist in the group, Deck Wilmouth, went up to the Matchless, and surprisingly, succeeded in getting his picture taken with Mrs. Baby Doe Tabor!

Another day, I was a member of a group taken through the Opera House by Tom Nicholas, an Elk member. I was thrilled with the idea of seeing the interior of this famous old building, then called the Elks' Opera House.

Entering through the front doors, I first noticed the abundant pictures of famous performers lining the foyer walls. Next, Mr. Nicholas led our group to the second floor to see the lodge rooms. There, he explained to us the details about the Elks' organization.

Then we descended the stairs to the theater level. At last, I was to see the auditorium! I could hardly wait while Mr. Nicholas tried out a number of keys from the ring he carried.

Soon, the huge auditorium doors were opened. It was quite dark in there, and a musty smell penetrated my nostrils, an odor typical of old buildings shut up for long periods. Despite the dimness and staleness, I swung my eyes around the enormous theater, trying to take in everything I could.

I shall never forget that first visit to the old Opera House. What a joy it was! Neither did I know, then, that someday many years later, my own mother was destined to purchase that very building! Nor did I dream that she and I would restore it, and open it for tours!

When that 1933 summer passed, I did not return to college as planned. In the spring of 1934, I married a Leadville man and settled down in a small cabin near the Silver Spoon Mine. This was several miles above the Matchless, where Baby Doe still lived, guarding that property.

My husband was one of a group that leased and worked the nearby Valley Mine. Incidentally, one man in this group used to leave his daily newspaper for Baby Doe, after he'd read it. As he passed by the Matchless, he would hand her the paper. She was always eager for the news. If he didn't see her around, he would leave it for her near the gate, covering it with a rock to keep it from blowing away.

How well I remember hearing about Baby Doe's death in 1935! It was a sad winter morning when the news spread that her frozen body had been found in her cabin.

I also recall the big snow of 1936. My husband and I were snowbound in our cabin from January until the last of March. To get groceries, my husband and other miners went to Leadville on snowshoes and skis. (Our car was parked beside the road near the cabin all winter, until a snow plow cleared the road in spring.)

To my amazement, it snowed every day the first three months of that year. The snowbanks were so high that the north window of our cabin was covered, completely.

It was dreadfully quiet up there in that cabin, when I was alone. I couldn't see anything outdoors but blowing snow, most of the time. On clear nights, I could look out the south window across the valley, afar, and see the bright lights of the Fortune Mine. And some nights, I could hear the spine-chilling cries of the

*The author pans for gold,
summer, 1933.*

*Author's husband, Gordon Furman,
feeds a chipmunk at The Silver Spoon
Mine cabin, 1934.*

Spring, 1936, after the heavy snowstorm, earlier. Picture taken from The Silver Spoon Mine dump above Leadville. In photo's center is The Valley Mine.

Evelyn Furman, standing in front of Mrs. Tabor's Matchless Mine cabin.

Evelyn E. Livingston Furman

Tabor Opera House Foyer. Behind counter, Evelyn Furman is selling books to tourists, 1971.

Theresa O'Brien, left, and Evelyn Furman, right, are homeward bound after a day of tours, 1971.

coyotes echoing through the cold crisp mountain air. How lonely Mrs. Tabor must have been, too, there all alone in her cabin during the long winters, previously.

This was a hard life for me, with no modern conveniences. "Why did I ever leave home?" was a question I asked myself often. I really should have finished college, as I had first intended.

In later years, my husband and I purchased an old house on East Ninth Street in Leadville. Boarded up for years, the house was filled with antique furniture, with everything in place just as it was left, years before, though covered with layers of fine dust.

Through the years, we moved several times until we finally found just the house we wanted; and my husband and I still occupy this Victorian home on Harrison Avenue. In 1937, I started a small furniture and appliance store, which kept me fully occupied.

Then came the purchase of the Tabor Opera House in 1955 by my mother! And I have dedicated the rest of my life to its restoration. Occasionally, I make the theater available to amateur theater groups who hold productions here.

It is my hope that future years will see continued preservation. And I await the day when the Tabor Opera House is restored to its former glory!

ABOUT THE AUTHOR:

Evelyn E. Livingston Furman descends from a long line of American pioneers. She came West as a young college student, and settled in Leadville, Colorado in 1933.

Deeply interested in Colorado history, she is especially fascinated with Leadville's history, so dear to her heart; and has been a collector of historical relics for many years. She has owned and operated Furman's Store since 1937. Greatly interested in mining, she also owns a number of Leadville mines. But most important of all, she is dedicated to a lifetime project: The restoration and preservation of the Tabor Opera House, and of her old Victorian home at 815 Harrison Avenue in Leadville.

Mrs. Furman's biography is listed in additional books as follows:
Who's Who of American Women, Marquis
Who's Who in the West, Marquis
Dictionary of International Biography, London
The Two Thousand Women of Achievement, London
World Who's Who in Finance and Industry, Marquis
National Social Directory
Personalities of the West and Midwest
Community Leaders of America
The National Register of Prominent Americans and International Notables

BIBLIOGRAPHY

History of Colorado by Frank Hall.
History of the Arkansas Valley-Part III, History of Lake County by R.G. Dill, published in 1881 by O.L. Baskin & Co., Chicago.
Tales of the Colorado Pioneers by Alice Polk Hill
Old items and photographs from the Author's collection, too numerous to mention.

I am also grateful to the Leadville people who furnished me with valuable information, and for the various newspaper articles saved, through the years.

> Evelyn E. Livingston Furman
> Leadville, Colorado

—1972.

PARTIAL DISCOGRAPHY OF PROGRAMS

Note: The following discography is by no means complete. Nonetheless, an attempt has been made to list as many shows as possible to those interested.

September 10, 1905—I.O.U., a musical satire; presented by Kolb and Dill.

September 19. 1905—A HUMAN SLAVE, melodrama.

September 26, 1905—DR. JEKYLL AND MR. HYDE, with Theo. Lorch; presented by Smutzer and Pelton.

October 5, 1905—THE TENDERFOOT, an operatic comedy, with Oscar L. Figman and Ruth White; presented by Oscar L. Figman.

October 8, 1905—CLEOPATRA IN HER PALACE OF ILLUSIONS; THE FLIGHT OF THE FAVORITE; HAPPENINGS IN THE SPOOK CAVE; THE FOUR AMERICAN TRUMPETERS; THE TROOPING OF THE COLORS; THE SLEEPING BEAUTY or a DREAM IN MID-AIR, with Adelaide Herrmann.

October 10, 1905—GHOSTS with Harry Mestayer; presented by Oliver Morosco.

November 8, 1905—WHITE TIGRESS OF JAPAN with Aileen May; presented by Charles D. Taylor.

November 22, 1905—THE KILTIES of Canada; B.D. Gilland, conductor.

December 10, 1905—FAMOUS GEORGIA MINSTRELS; presented by Richards & Pringle.

January 1, 1906—NEW LONDON GAIETY GIRLS; presented by Nettie Grant.

January 7, 1906—MINERS' MERRY BURLESQUERS present A NIGHT ON THE BOWERY, a musical comedy.

January 19, 1906—OLE OLSON with Ben Hendricks and company.

January 21, 1906—THE MERCHANT OF VENICE with Charles B. Hanford and Miss Marie Drofnah.

February 8, 1906—A PAIR OF PINKS with Margaret Daly Vokes.

February 12, 1906—COUSIN KATE with Alberta Gallatin.

February 27, 1906—CAPTAIN DEBONNAIRE, a romantic drama, with Paul Gilmore.

April 2, 1906—THE LIFE OF DORA THORNE, a rural English comedy; presented by Rowland and Clifford.

April 3, 1906—THE BONNIE BRIER BUSH, drama by Ian Maclaren; presented by Ernest Shipman and William G. Colvin.

April 6, 1906—THE JEFFERSON FARM by the Frontier Company.

April 7, 1906—ALICE-SIT-BY-THE-FIRE with Roselle Knott and players.

April 7, 1906—ON THE FRONTIER by the Frontier Company.

April 8, 1906—CLOVERDALE by the Frontier Company.

April 21, 1906—HER DOUBLE LIFE with Miss Laura Frankenfield and company; presented by Leon A. Gilson.

April 23, 1906—KNOBS OF TENNESSEE with the Kempton Komedy Ko.

April 24, 1906—FOR HEARTH AND HOME with the Kempton Komedy Ko.

April 25, 1906—IN DARKEST RUSSIA with the Kempton Komedy Ko.

June 7, 1906—WEDDED, BUT NO WIFE with the Kempton Komedy Ko.

June 8, 1906—JERRY, THE TRAMP with the Kempton Komedy Ko.

June 9, 1906—THE CORNER GROCERY with the Kempton Komedy Ko.

June 10, 1906—MRS. WARREN'S PROFESSION by George Bernard Shaw, with Miss Rose Coghlan.

July 16, 1906—LITTLE TORMENT with Arington's Comedians.

July 17, 1906—OLD KENTUCKY with Arington's Comedians.

July 18, 1906—GOLDEN GIANT MINE with Arington's Comedians.

July 19, 1906—KATHLEEN MAVOUREEN or THE MYSTERY OF THE BLACK CRAG with Arington's Comedians.

August 10, 1906—LEAH, THE FORSAKEN with Arington's Comedians.

August 11, 1906—SANDY BOTTOM with Arington's Comedians.

August 12, 1906—AT CRIPPLE CREEK or THE PARSON'S CLAIM with Arington's Comedians.

August 19, 1906—THE DOWNWARD PATH or MAN'S ENEMY with the Kempton Komedy Ko.

August 20, 1906—A WOMAN'S SACRIFICE with the Kempton Komedy Ko.

August 21, 1906—MONTE CRISTO with the Kempton Komedy Ko.

August 22, 1906—A GREAT WRONG RIGHTED with the Kempton Komedy Ko.

August 23, 1906—PAWN TICKET 210 OR THE LIVING PLEDGE with the Kempton Komedy Ko.

August 24, 1906—THE TWO ORPHANS with the Kempton Komedy Ko.

August 25, 1906—WOMAN AGAINST WOMAN with the Kempton Komedy Ko.

August 26, 1906—THE PRIVATE SECRETARY with the Kempton Komedy Ko.

September 2, 1906—THE WIZARD OF WALL STREET

September 4, 1906—BEYOND THE LAW with the Kempton Komedy Ko.

September 5, 1906—THE HAND OF MAN with the Kempton Komedy Ko.

September 6, 1906—FOR HOME AND HONOR with the Kempton Komedy Ko.

September 6, 1906—HUMAN HEARTS with the Kempton Komedy Ko.

September 7, 1906—IN THE SHADOW OF THE GALLOWS or THE BLACK FLAG with the Kempton Komedy Ko.

September 9, 1906—THE HOLY CITY OF JERUSALEM

September 10, 1906—THE LIEUTENANT AND THE COWBOY with Theodore Lorch; presented by Messrs. Felton & Smutzer.

September 15, 1906—A ROYAL SLAVE presented by Gordon and Bennett.

September 17, 1906—A MILLIONAIRE TRAP presented by Elmer Walters.

September 20, 1906—THE HOLY CITY with Luella Morey; presented by LeComte & Flesher.

September 23, 1906—THE FREEDOM OF SUZANNE with Jane Corcoran; presented by Arthur C. Aiston

September 24, 1906—PETER PETERSON or CHRISTIAN COUNTRY FOLKS.

September 29, 1906—A DESERTED BRIDE by Fitzgerald Murphy; directed by George Samuels.

October 3, 1906—A MESSAGE FROM MARS presented by A.L. Rheinstrom

October 3, 1906—THE ALASKAN, an original comic opera; presented by John Cort.

October 6, 1906—THE ROYAL CHEF, a musical comedy; presented by Frazee and Wade.

October 11, 1906—THE YANKEE REGENT, a musical; presented by H.H. Frazee with Toby Lyons.

October 12, 1906—ARIZONA; presented by Hollis E. Cooley.

October 15, 1906—THE GIRL AND THE BANDIT, a comedy opera; presented by the Viola Gillette Opera Co.

October 15, 1906—THE STRONGER SEX, a comedy by John Valentine, with Maude Fealy.

October 16, 1906—THE GIRL AND THE BANDIT, a comedy opera, with the Viola Gillette Opera Co.; directed by Hugh A. Grady.

October 17, 1906—MAHARA'S MINSTRELS.

October 19, 1906—PEGGY FROM PARIS, a musical, with Arthur Deagon; presented by Madison Corey.

October 21, 1906—PECK'S BAD BOY, a comedy, presented by the Union Amusement Co. of New York.

October 24, 1906—BENEFIT CONCERT by Miss Austin.

October 28, 1906—ROYAL HAWAIIAN BAND from Hawaii; presented by J.C. Cohen.

October 29, 1906—HIS HIGHNESS, THE BEY or THE ROAD TO MANDALAY.

October 30, 1906—HI HENRY'S GREATEST MINSTRELS.

November 7, 1906—PARSIFAL, presented by Messrs. Martin and Mery.

November 15, 1906—THE MAN ON THE BOX, a comedy, with Max Figman.

November 16, 1906—THE DEVIL'S AUCTION; directed by Charles H. Yale.

November 18, 1906—THE MAID AND THE MUMMY.

November 20, 1906—THE MISSOURI GIRL, a comedy by Fred Raymond.

December 6, 1906—THE WHITE SLAVE with Georgia Harper and Co.; with Joseph Newman and Inez Brown.

December 16, 1906—BUSTER BROWN with Master Percy Helton as Buster; presented by the Buster Brown Amusement Co.

December 23, 1906—UNCLE JOSH PERKINS.

December 26, 1906—THE SULTAN OF SULU.

December 27, 1906—THE ILLUSION OF BEATRICE, a comedy, with Maude Fealy; presented by John Cort.

December 30, 1906—MY WIFE'S FAMILY, a musical farce comedy; presented by William McGowan.

January 1, 1907—THE SIGN OF THE CROSS, a religious drama; presented by Wilson Barrett.

January 6, 1907—DOROTHY VERNON OF HADDON HALL, a romantic play, with Alberta Gallatin; presented by Sweely, Shipman and Co.

January 9, 1907—THE SIGN OF THE FOUR with the Theodore Lorch Co.

January 13, 1907—RED FEATHER, a romantic opera by DeKoven, Klein and Cook; with Cheridah Simpson.

January 15, 1907—THE STRENGTH OF THE WEAK with Florence Roberts.

January 22, 1907—UNDER SOUTHERN SKIES by Lottie Glair Parker.

January 24, 1907—RICHARD THE THIRD with tragedian John Griffith.

January 31, 1907—KERRY GOW with Allen Doone.

February 4, 1907—AT YALE, with Paul Gilmore; presented by Jules Murry.

February 12, 1907—SERGEANT KITTY with Miss Helen Byron; presented by C. Weis.

March 13, 1907—THE TENDERFOOT, a western operatic comedy, with Oscar L. Figman and Ruth White; presented by William P. Cullen.

April 28, 1907—$10,000 BEAUTY, a musical comedy, with Allen Curtis and Co.

April 30, 1907—JULIUS CAESAR with Charles B. Hanford and Miss Marie Drofnah; directed by F. Lawrence Walker

May 10, 1907—A COUNTRY GIRL with the Augustin Daly Musical Co.

May 11, 1907—THE CINGALEE with the Augustin Daly Musical Co.

May 14, 1907—WHAT A NEWSPAPER MAN SAW IN PANAMA with 15 moving pictures and 20 lantern slides.

June 5, 1907—FROM RAGS TO RICHES with the Kempton Komedy Ko.

June 6, 1907—A HOME SPUN HEART with the Kempton Komedy Ko.

July 21, 1907—THE CHORUS GIRL, a comedy-drama; presented by the Della Pringle Stock Co.

July 22, 1907—THE LIGHT HOUSE ROBBERY presented by the Della Pringle Stock Co.

July 23, 1907—HER MAD MARRIAGE, a melodrama; presented by the Della Pringle Stock Co.

July 24, 1907—THE GALLEY SLAVE, a society drama; presented by the Della Pringle Stock Co.

July 25, 1907—THE VILLAGE PEACEMAKER presented by the Della Pringle Stock Co.

July 26, 1907—A KENTUCKY GIRL presented by the Della Pringle Stock Co.

July 27, 1907—DANGERS OF A GREAT CITY presented by the Della Pringle Stock Co.

July 28, 1907—THE LITTLE DETECTIVE presented by the Della Pringle Stock Co.

July 29, 1907—THE GALLEY SLAVE presented by the Della Pringle Stock Co.

July 30, 1907—HER MAD MARRIAGE presented by the Della Pringle Stock Co.

July 31, 1907—A SOUTHERN ROMANCE presented by the Della Pringle Stock Co.

August 1, 1907—THE PARISH PRIEST presented by the Della Pringle Stock Co.

February 6, 1908—THE MAN ON THE BOX with Max Figman; presented by John Cort.

February 13, 1908—MA'S NEW HUSBAND presented by the Harry Scott Amusement Co.

February 17, 1908—THE WHEEL OF LOVE with Paul Gilmore; presented by Jules Murry.

February 20, 1908—WAY DOWN EAST produced by William A. Brady.

February 25, 1908—MRS. WARREN'S PROFESSION by George Bernard Shaw, with Miss Mary Shaw and Co.; presented by Ernest Shuter.

March 12, 1908—BUSTER BROWN, a cartoon comedy, with Master Rice as Buster; presented by The Buster Brown Amusement Co.

March 15, 1908—PAINTING THE TOWN, a musical, by W.F. Carroll; presented by Charles H. Yale.

March 18, 1808—THE BONDMAN with Wilton Lackaye; presented by William A. Brady.

March 20, 1908—THE GINGERBREAD MAN with the Nixon and Simmerman Co., by Frederick Hankin and A. Baldwin Sloane.

March 22, 1908—QUINCY ADAMS SAWYER managed by John G. Stewart.

April 7, 1908—ANTONY AND CLEOPATRA with Charles B. Hanford managed by F. Lawrence Walker.

April 9, 1908—ZIRA with Florence Roberts; presented by Henry B. Harris and John Cort.

April 13, 1908—DREAM CITY with Little Chip and Mary Marble; produced by Joe Weber.

April 19, 1908—MRS. TEMPLE'S TELEGRAM presented by Messrs. Stockwell and McGregor.

May 3, 1908—THE BLACK CROOK with H.E. Willard; presented by Miller and Plohn.

June 6, 1908—THE GREAT DIVIDE with Henry Miller.

August 24, 1908—MY DIXIE GIRL with the Kempton Komedy Ko.

August 26, 1908—A TEXAS RANGER, a romantic drama, with the Kempton Komedy Ko.

August 26, 1908 and August 29, 1908—MORE TO BE PITIED THAN SCORNED with the Kempton Komedy Ko.

August 27, 1908—MY FRIEND FROM ARKANSAW - with the Kempton Komedy Ko.

August 28, 1908—DANIEL BOONE ON THE TRAIL, a historical comedy drama, with the Kempton Komedy Ko.

August 29. 1908—THE WORLD or THE STRUGGLE FOR LIFE; with the Kempton Komedy Ko.

August 30, 1908—THE TIE THAT BINDS, a society drama, with the Kempton Komedy Ko.

September 13, 1908—THE ROYAL CHEF, a musical comedy, presented by H.H. Frazee.

September 30, 1908—HANS & NIX, a musical gaiety, with Dixon and Bernard.

October 7, 1908—THE BURGOMASTER presented by William P. Cullen.

October 23, 1908—THE CAT AND THE FIDDLE presented by Charles A. Sellon.

October 29, 1908—TEXAS, a romantic comedy.

October 31, 1908—UNCLE TOM'S CABIN by Stetson.

November 11, 1908—A KNIGHT FOR A DAY presented by H.H. Frazee.

November 15, 1908—PARSIFAL presented by Messrs. Martin and Emery.

November 20, 1908—THE SUNNY SIDE OF BROADWAY with Charles A. Murray and Ollie Mack.

November 26, 1908—ISLE OF SPICE presented by H.H. Frazee.

November 30, 1908—NATURE'S NOBLEMAN with the Marie Fountain Theater Co.

December 1, 1908—JIM, THE WESTERNER with the Marie Fountain Theater Co.

December 2, 1908—ADRIFT IN NEW YORK with the Marie Fountain Theater Co.

December 3, 1908—HOME SWEET HOME with the Marie Fountain Theater Co.

December 4, 1908—FATAL ROSES with the Marie Fountain Theater Co.

December 5, 1908—BEYOND THE LAW with the Marie Fountain Theater Co.

December 6, 1908—KU KLUX KLAN with Marie Fountain Theater Co.

December 9, 1908—BREWSTER'S MILLIONS with Robert Ober, by Frederick Thompson, producer, and The Cohan and Harris Comedians.

December 11, 1908—RUNNING FOR OFFICE or THE HONEYMOONERS presented by Hope and Welch.

December 18, 1908—THE NIGHT OF THE PLAY with comedienne Kathryn Osterman.

December 22, 1908—JUST OUT OF COLLEGE, a modern light comedy with music; presented by George Ade.

January 5, 1909—THE WOLF, a melodrama, by the Lyric Theater.

January 6, 1909—THE SUBSTITUTE, a comedy drama, with Max Figman; presented by John Cort.

January 24, 1909—SIS HOPKINS with comedienne Rose Melville; presented by J.R. Stirling.

January 27, 1909—IN WYOMING presented by H.E. Pierce and Co.

February 10, 1909—SHORE ACRES with Archie Boyd; presented by Charles A. Miller, Inc.

February 16, 1909—THE HOUSE OF BONDAGE with Florence Roberts; presented by John Cort.

February 25, 1909—THE HOLY CITY with Puella Morey; presented by LeComte and Flesher.

March 1, 1909—THE RIGHT OF WAY with Standing and Roberts; presented by Klaw and Erlanger.

March 2, 1909—RIP VAN WINKLE with Thomas Jefferson.

March 30, 1909—BABES IN TOYLAND.

April 13, 1909—THE WINTER'S TALE with Charles B. Hanford and Miss Marie Drofnah.

April 21, 1909—THE BURGOMASTER presented by William P. Cullen.

July 30, 1909—PAID IN FULL with the Wagenhals and Kemper Co.

September 15, 1909—THE ALASKAN, a musical comedy, presented by William P. Cullen.

September 22, 1909—LENA RIVERS with Emma Bunting; presented by Barton and Wiswell Co., Inc.

September 28, 1909—HONEYMOON TRIAL presented by the Princess Amusement Co.

September 26, 1909—THE CAT AND THE FIDDLE.

October 15, 1909—THE GIRL FROM RECTORS.

October 19, 1909—VASTA HERNE with Mrs. Leslie Carter.

November 2, 1909—A KNIGHT FOR A DAY presented by H.H. Frazee.

November 3, 1909—A GENTLEMAN FROM MISSISSIPPI presented by Messrs. William A. Brady and Joseph R. Grismer.

November 15, 1909—THE SOUL KISS presented by The Soul Kiss Co., Inc.

November 18, 1909—THE TIME, THE PLACE AND THE GIRL, a comedy with music; presented by H.H. Frazee, Inc.

November 19, 1909—THE GIRL QUESTION presented by H.H. Frazee, Inc.

November 28, 1909—LO with John E. Young; presented by The Harry Askin Co., Inc.

December 1, 1909—COMMENCEMENT DAYS with Frederick V. Bowers; presented by John Cort.

December 30, 1909—LITTLE JOHNNY JONES presented by the Colonial Amusement Co.

January 1, 1910—HUMAN HEARTS presented by W.E. Hankeville.

January 5, 1910—THE VIRGINIAN presented by The Kirke La Shelle Co.

January 13, 1910—WILDFIRE, the great racing comedy.

January 21. 1910—IN WYOMING presented by H.E. Pierce and Co.

January 27, 1910—HAMLET, PRINCE OF DENMARK with Robert Mantell; presented by William A. Brady.

February 2, 1910—KING DODO, a comedy opera, presented by John Cort.

February 9, 1910—THE LAND OF NOD, a musical extravaganza, presented by Samuel S. Rork.

February 15, 1910—THE ALASKAN presented by William P. Cullen.

February 17, 1910—THE HOUSE OF A THOUSAND CANDLES presented by W.T. Gaskell and Edward Rowland.

February 22, 1910—THE TOP OF THE WORLD with Bailey & Austin; presented by George H. Murray.

March 11, 1910—MARY JANE'S PA with Max Figman; presented by John Cort.

March 17, 1910—BREWSTER'S MILLIONS with Royal Tracy, George M. Cohan and Sam H. Harris comedians.

March 30, 1910—THE GREAT DIVIDE presented by Henry Miller.

April 5, 1910—THE AMERICAN LORD, a modern comedy, with Charles B. Hanford and Miss Marie Drofnah.

April 23, 1910—WIDOW JONES with prima donna comedienne Dorothy Morton; presented by G.L. Briggs.

June 7, 1910—St. Mary's School, Leadville, Colorado.

PAST PERFORMERS

Following is a partial list, at random, of the actors and actresses who appeared at the Tabor Opera House in myriad performances:

Maud Adams
Chauncy Alcott
Blanch Aldrock
Will Archie
Arington's Comedians
Lawrence Barrett
Louis Beaudet
Rev. Henry Ward Beecher
Big Jubilee Minstrels
Max Bloom
Dion Boucicault
Sophie Brandt
William Burroughs
Helen Byron
Callender Minstrels, The
J.H. Campbell
Creston Clarke
Harry Corson Clarke
Kate Claxton
Effie Coghlan
Samuel Collins
Joseph Conyers
Jane Corcoran
Eugene Cowles
Lotta Crabtree
William H. Crane
Creatore and His Italian Band
Frank Daniels
E.L. Davenport
Jefferson De Angeles
Dockstader Minstrels, The
Allen Doone
Marie Drofnah
Arthur Dunn
Dustin Farnum
Maude Fealy
Oscar Figman
Mrs. Fiske
Florence Gale
Alberta Gallatin
Edward Garvie
William Gibson

Viola Gillette
William Gillette
Paul Gilmore
Charles B. Hanford
Georgia Harper
Edward Harrington
Haverly's Mastodon Minstrels
Anna Held
Ben Hendricks
Henry Horton
Houdini, the Magician
T.C. Howard
Charles Hoyt
Louis James
Madame Janausckek
James J. Jeffries
Alice Johnston
John Kelly
Lillian Kimble
Roselle Knott
Howard Kyle
Jack S. Langrishe
Harry Lauder
Jeanette Lincoln
London Gaiety Girls
James B. Mackie
Florence Martin
Robert Mantell
Richard Mansfield
John Mason
Phosa McAllister
Steele McKaye
Rose Melville
Metropolitan Opera Co.
Helen Modjeska
Guissepina Moracchi
Lewis Morrison
Joseph Murphy
National Grand Opera Co.
Milton Nobles
Rhen Nores
Lillian Olcott

Daphne Pollard
Helen Prime
George Primrose and His Minstrel Co.
David Proctor
Kate Putnam
Will Rising
Florence Roberts
Gladys Robeson
Stuart Robson
Frank Roche
Lillian Russell
Charles A. Sellon
Otis Skinner
John Philip Sousa
Ogden Stevens
Ralph Stewart
J.H. Stoddart

Fred Stone
E.P. Sullivan
Daniel Sully
Bert Swor
Otis B. Thayer
Augustus Thomas
J.C. Turner
W.H. Turner
Dorothy Vernon
Charles Vivian
Blanch Walsh
Frederic Warde
White Whittlesey
Oscar Wilde
Franker Woods
John E. Young
Zamlock, the Magician

ACTORS AND ACTRESSES

From the Author's Collection

Will Archie

Max Bloom

Helen Byron

Creston Clarke

Samuel Collins in "The Silver Slipper"

Joseph Conyers

102

Charles B. Hanford, early-day actor who appeared at The Tabor Opera House.

Marie Drofnah, actress and wife of Charles B. Hanford. Note that "Drofnah" is Hanford" spelled backwards.

Anna Held. Photographer: Reutlinger, 21 Boulevard Montmartre, Paris.

John Philip Sousa

Mrs. Fiske

Mrs. Leslie Carter

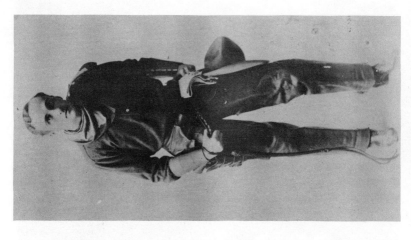

William Gibson as "The Virginian"

106

Jane Corcoran

Eugene Cowles

fferson De Angeles in "The Beauty
ot"102-98

Allen Doone

107

Erb & Stanley

Dustin Farnum

Maude Fealy

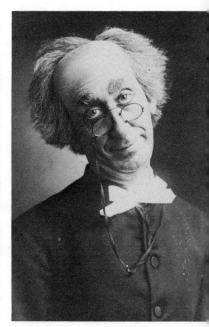

Oscar Figman

Alberta Gallatin *Edward Garvie*

iola Gillette in ''The Beauty Spot'' *Paul Gilmore*

109

Ben Hendricks

Alice Johnston

Kathryn Kidder in "Salammbo"

Roselle Knott

Howard Kyle as Sir Jasper Thorndye
in "Rosemary."

Robert Mantell

Florence Martin in "The Beauty Spot"

John Mason in "The Witching Hour"

Rose Melville

Lewis Morrison

Chauncy Olcott

Daphne Pollard

Helen Prime

George Primrose

David Proctor

Florence Roberts

Charles A. Sellon

Otis Skinner as "Hamlet"

Ogden Stevens

J.H. Stoddart in "Bonnie Brier"

Bert Swor and Franker Woods in
"Red Mill"

Ralph Stuart

J.C. Turner

W.H. Turner as "David Harum"

Blanche Walsh

White Whittlessey

Fredrick Warde in "Salammbo"
October 22, 1904.

Fredrick Ward and Louis James in
"Alexander The Great" October 26, 19

116

Programs

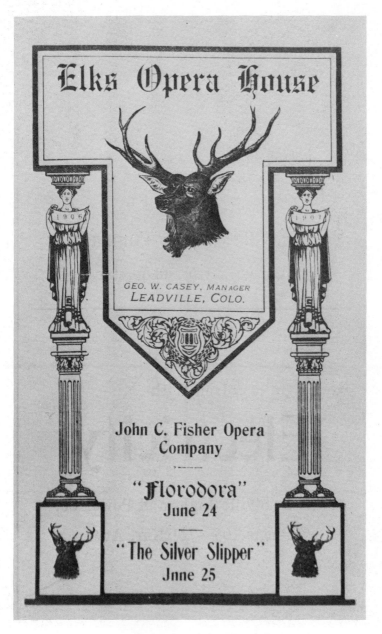

"Florodora" and *"The Silver Slipper"*

PROGRAM.

MR. JOHN C. FISHER
Presents

"The Silver Slipper"
JUNE 25

Lyrics by W. H. RISQUE
Music by Leslie Stuart
Book by Owen Hall

CAST OF CHARACTERS

HENRY BISMARK HENCHES,
showman, card sharp and all around
fakir.   GEO. E. MACK
Sir Victor Schallamer, an astronomer,
Joseph Monahan
Berkley Schallamer, of the household
brigade, nephew of Sir Victor
Arthur Deane
Donald Gregor of the Royal Navy
Geo. E. Whyte
Duval   Geo. B. Jackson

Get the Habit—A Trip to Leon's
After the Show.

PAGE THREE

118

PROGRAM — (Continued)

Roland Western............Edward Hemmer
Gen. D'Arme................Thos. W. Lane
Wrenne.................Gertrude Millington
Belle Jimper, servant of Sir Victor
..................................Julia Folland
Stella, the girl from Venice..Julia Frary
Brenda, niece of Sir Victor......
..................................Agnes Finley
Susette................Lolita Gordon
Dolly, the maid........Olive Roberts
Butler.......................J. Quinn
Astria....................Eva Abbott
Dione....................Helen Keers
Ira....................Crosby Little
Cleo................Nancy Nathaway
Lydia..................Maude Jones
Gillian................Helen Rousseau
  Chorus of Students. Gen. D'Armes,
Flower Girls, Waiters and Attendants
by the Chorus. Ladies of the Ballet,
Misses Roberts, Walker, Loraine and
Astor.
  MUSICAL NUMBERS
  Max Winne, Director of Music
  ACT I— Opening Chorus, Students.
2—Tonight's the Night, Joseph Mona-

PAGE FOUR.

PROGRAM — (Continued)

han. 3—Soldiers of the Army. Arthur Deane. 4—Two Eyes of Blue, Geo. Whyte. 5—You and Me, Gertrude Millington and Arthur Deane. 6—Finale, Ensemble.

ACT II—7—Opening Chorus, Chorus. 8—The Baby with the Dimple and the Smile, Gertrude Millington. 9—Prosperity, Geo. E. Mack. 10—Duet, The Dawn of Love, Julia Frary and Geo. E. Whyte. 11—The Champagne Dance, Misses Olive Roberts, Camille Astor, Alma Loraine and Rita Walker. 12—The Girl You Love, Gertrude Millington.

BALL ROOM SCENE

13—Dance, Slow Waltz, The Dancing Girls. 14—Tessie, Geo. E. Whyte. 15—Four and Twenty Little Men, Gertrude Millington. 16—Class, Julia Folland. 17—Finale, Ensemble.

SYNOPSIS—Act I—The Garden of the College of Sir Victor Schallamar. Act II—Scene 1—Neuilly Fair, France. Scene 2—Students' Ball at the Art Club, Paris.

Get the Habit—A Trip to Leon's After the Show.

PAGE FIVE.

PROGRAM — (Continued)

MR. JOHN C. FISHER

Presents

THE POPULAR MUSIC COMEDY

"FLORODORA"

JUNE 24

Lyric by Owen Hall

Music by Leslie Stuart

CAST OF CHARACTERS

Cyrus Gilfain, proprietor of the Island
  and Perfume of Florodora............
..........................Joseph Monahan
Captain Arthur Donegal, Lady Holy-
  rood's brother............Geo. Whyte
Frank Abercoed, Gilfain's manager....
..........................Arthur Deane
Leandro, overseer of farms............
..........................Geo. B. Jackson

Diamonds, watches, jewelry, cut glass
—F. J. Mund's.

PAGE SIX.

PROGRAM — (Continued)

Gilfain's Clerks:—

Tennyson Sims	Harry St. Clair
Ernest Pym	Edward Hemmer
Max Aptelbaum	Fred Jones
Reginald Langdale	Peter Gellispie
Paul Crogan	Harry Edwards
John Scott	William Baker
William, a footman	Thos. Lane

Anthony Tweedlepunch, showman, phrenologist, hypnotist and palmist
GEORGE E. MACK

Dolores	Julia Frary
Valleda, a maid	Olive Roberts

Florodora Girls:—

Inez	Rita Walker
Jose	Leonora Walters
Juanita	Iren Ashby
Violante	Alma Loraine
Calixta	Maude Cannar
Mica	Camille Astor
Angela Gilfain	Agnes Finley

English Guests of Mr. Gilfain's daughter:—

Get a nice warm drink at Leon's before going home.

PAGE SEVEN.

PROGRAM — (Continued)

Daisy Chain	Helen Rousseau
Mamie Rowe	Crosby Little
Lucy Ring	Lolita Gordon
Cynthia Chalmers	Eva Abbott
Clara Fitzgerald	Nancy Nathaway
Cynthia Belmont	Nellie Keers
Lady Holyrood	Gertrude Millington
Florodora Farmers, Laborers, Flower Girls, Welsh Peasants, etc.	

MUSICAL NUMBERS

Max Winne, Director of Music

ACT I—1—Opening Chorus. 2—Sextette, "The Credit's Due to Me," Clerks and Chorus. 3—Duet, "Somebody," Dolores and Abercoed. 4—Chorus of Welcome. 5—Concerted number. "Come and See Our Island." 6—Song. "When I Leave Town," Lady Holyrood. 7—Duet, "Galloping," Angela and Denegal. 8—Trio, "I want to Marry a Man, I Do," Lady Holyrood, Tweedlepunch and Gilfain. 9—Song, "Phrenology," Gilfain and Chorus. 10—Song, "The Shade of the Palm," Ab-

---

PAGE EIGHT.

PROGRAM — (Continued)

ercoed. 11—Finale, Chorus and Principals of company.

ACT II—12—Opening Chorus. 13—Song and Chorus, "Tact," Lady Holyrood and Chorus. 14—Song, "The Millionaire," Gilfain and Chorus. 15—Concerted number—double sextette—"Tell Me, Pretty Maiden," English Girls and Gilfain's Clerks. 16—Duet, "We Get Up at 8 a. m.," Valleda and Leandro. 17—Song. "The Fellow who Might," Angella. 18—Duet, "We're Both on the Stage," Dolores and Tweedlepunch. 19—Song, "I'd Like to Marry You," Lady Holyrood. 20—Song, "The Queen of the Philippine Islands," Dolores. 21—Song, "I Want to be a Military Man," Donegal and Chorus. 22—Finale, Entire Company.

SYNOPSIS

Act I—Island of 'Florodora, Philippines. Act II—Scene 1—Abercoed Castle, Wales. Scene 2—Ball Room of Abercoed Castle.

Get the Habit—A Trip to Leon's After the Show.

PAGE NINE.

124

125

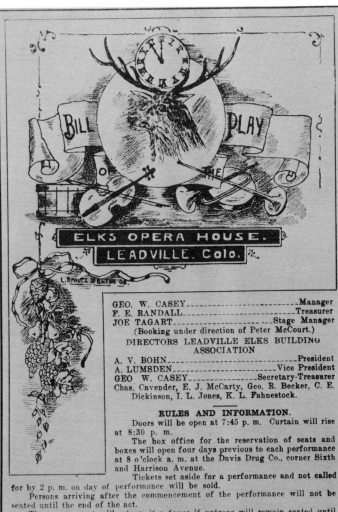

GEO. W. CASEY_____Manager
F. E. RANDALL_____Treasurer
JOE TAGART_____Stage Manager
(Booking under direction of Peter McCourt.)
DIRECTORS LEADVILLE ELKS BUILDING
ASSOCIATION
A. V. BOHN_____President
A. LUMSDEN_____Vice President
GEO W. CASEY_____Secretary-Treasurer
Chas. Cavender, E. J. McCarty, Geo. R. Becker, C. E.
Dickinson, I. L. Jones, K. L. Fahnestock.

RULES AND INFORMATION.

Doors will be open at 7:45 p. m. Curtain will rise
at 8:30 p. m.

The box office for the reservation of seats and
boxes will open four days previous to each performance
at 8 o'clock a. m. at the Davis Drug Co., corner Sixth
and Harrison Avenue.

Tickets set aside for a performance and not called
for by 2 p. m. on day of performance will be sold.

Persons arriving after the commencement of the performance will not be
seated until the end of the act.

The management will esteem it a favor if patrons will remain seated until
the final fall of the curtain, and requests that the adjusting of hats and wraps
may be deferred until program is quite finished.

Any difficulty arising in respect to errors in tickets or sittings should be
referred to the management for speedy and proper adjustment.

Ladies' retiring room and toilet will be found to the left. Check room for
wraps, etc., will be found to the right. No charge will be made for checking.

Physicians and others anticipating calls during the performance should
leave their seat location and name at the door.

The management requests that ladies will kindly not wear their hats in
any part of the theater.

"Peer Gynt"

127

PROGRAM

SATURDAY, NOVEMBER 14, 1908

LOUIS JAMES

supported by

APHIE JAMES

and his Company presenting Henrik Ibsen's Comedy or Human Life

"PEER GYNT"

Management of Wallace Munro.

DRAMATIS PERSONAE

Peer Gynt _____ Louis James
Ase, his mother __ Laura Frankenfield
Aslak, the blacksmith__Norman Sweet
Mads Moen, the bridegroom _____
_____ Arthur Weston
His Father _____ James Robertson
His Mother _____ Mary Bernard
Solveig _____ Aphie James
Helga, her sister ____ A. Belle Keefe
Their Father _____ Kraft Walton
Their Mother _____ Margaret Warren
The Hegstad Farmer _____
_____ Frank C. Chapman
Ingrid, the bride; his daughter ____

PROGRAM—Continued.

	Ida Werner
First Peasant Lad	Hugh H. Lindsay
Second Peasant Lad	Henry Hempel
Third Peasant Lad	Louis G. Reynolds
Fourth Peasant Lad	George Loomis
First Peasant Girl	Myrtle Webster
Second Peasant Girl	Elsie Scharff
Third Peasant Girl	Josephine Leon
Fiddler	A. B. Frederick
Mr. Cotton	J. Arthur Young
Monsieur Ballon	Wm. C. Andrews
Herr Von Eberkopf	Kraft Walton
Herr Trumpeterstrale	
	Richard I. Scott
Waiter	Arthur Wardner
Anitra	Frances Harcourt
Captain of the Ship	James G. Howe
Boatswain	R. D. Sanderson
Bailiff	Alden Jewell

Wedding Guests, Peasants, Lads, Girls
Dancing Girls, the Ship's crew and
others.

2

129

PROGRAM—Continued.

SUPERNATURAL BEINGS

The Green Clad Woman _____
_____ Anne Schaefer
The King of the Trolls _____
_____ J. Arthur Young
First Troll Imp _____ Harold Forrest
Second Troll Imp __ James McDonald
Third Troll Imp _____ Charles Archer
The Ugly Brat _____ Vera Walton
The Boyg _____ F. A. Browne
The Strange Passenge (Wm. C. Andrews
The Button Moulder   (
Troll Courtiers, Imps and Troll Maidens.

THE SCENES
PART ONE

ACT I—Scene 1—Norway. The Mill House. Gynt's Home. Scene 2—Hegstad Farm.
ACT II—Scene 1—In the Mountains. Scene 2—The Hall of the Dovre King. Scene 3—In the Mountains.
ACT III—Scene 1—Peer's Hut in the Forest. Scene 2—The Interior of Gynt's Home.
PART TWO
ACT IV—Scene 1—Norway. A Vision of Solveig Waiting. Scene 2—

PROGRAM—Continued.

Morocco. A Palm Grove on the Coast
 ACT V—Scene 1—On Board a Ship in the North Sea. Scene 2—Norway. Solveig's Hut.
 Thirty years are supposed to have elapsed between Part I and II.

SYNOPSIS
PART ONE

ACT 1—Scene 1—Peer Gynt at his home in the mountains with his mother. This scene displays Peer Gynt as the untrained mind, the unconscious dreamer, a poet and the reckless hobbledehoy. It also indicates his aspirations to be a ruler among men.

Scene 2—Peer Gynt attends the wedding festivities at Hagstadt, and meets Solveig. He is poor and shabby, but aspiring and dreaming of great things. He is scoffed and derided by all. He becomes more and more reckless; drinks to excess, and thinking himself slighted by Solveig, with whom he has fallen in love, he steals the bride out of sheer bravado and escapes to the mountains with her.

PROGRAM—Continued.

ACT II—Scene 1—Sick of the adventure he curtly dismisses Ingrid, the bride. He is haunted by the farmers and peasants, and, completely exhausted and worn out by the fatigue and dissipation, sinks into a stupor.

Scene 2—In his distorted fancy he is visited by the Dovre King's daughter, and goes with her to the court of the King of Trolls. Crying to his mother for help, the Trolls flee and Peer Gynt is left alone in the darkness, to an encounter with the Great Boyg. The liquor''s effect passing off, he awakes and finds Solveig and her little sister Helga watching him, but they flee and he is again left alone.

ACT III—Scene 1—Peer Gynt, undaunted, builds himself a hut, and, outlawed, prepares to lead the life of a hermit, but Solveig, who has loved him at first sight, comes to him in the forest to dwell with him there; Gynt's dream of happiness is dispelled by the appearance of the Dovre King's daughter who threatens to ever stand between him and Solveig, and hopelessly

PROGRAM—Continued.

discouraged, Peer departs, bidding her wait for him.

Scene 2—Seeking for comfort, Peer returns to his mother's hut, only to find her dying. Leaving her dead, he fares across seas.

PART TWO

ACT IV—Scene 1—(A Vision) Thirty years have elapsed, and Solveig is disclosed waiting and ever waiting for Peer.

Scene 2—Peer has become very wealthy, and a man of the world. He visits the coast of Morocco with a band of friends. He announces to them his intention to become emperor of the world, but they steal his yacht and leave him. The yacht is destroyed. Peer, meantime has fallen a victim to the wiles of Anitra, a dancing girl, who has stolen his wealth and sent him adrift. She celebrates her conquest in a dance and song, accompanied by her troupe of maiden attendants.

ACT V—Scene 1—Embarking on a Norwegian vessel, bound for his old home, his ship encounters a violent storm, and strikes a rock and sinks. Peer has grown old and worn, and for

6

PROGRAM—Continued.

the first time meets the dread messenger.

Scene 2—An auction is in progress near the old cottage, and thither Peer Gynt comes after the shipwreck, feeble and almost demented. All his dreams and aspirations are now threadbare. He encounters his old friends the Dovre King and Button Moulder, and in vain searches everywhere for rest and salvation. From the old hut, Solveig comes to him, and in her love he finally finds refuge, peace and happiness.

This phantasmagoria, or comedy of human life, embraces all the elements of the serious, the pathetic, the tragic, the grotesque, the real and the unreal, the actualities and the dreams, the facts and the consequences, the ambitions and the disappointments, the hopes and the disillusions, and the dread and terror, and the resurrection, in love, of the human soul.

The music, mainly on themes from Edward Grieg's "Peer Gynt" suites, is arranged by Clarence Lucas, the scenery is painted by Frank Platzer, and built by T. B. McDonald, the production staged by Frederick Paulding.

7

ORCHESTRA UNDER THE DIRECTION OF THEO. L. CURRIE

Selection, Peer Gynt _____ C. Lucas
The Morning _____ E. Grieg
March Triumphal _____ E. Grieg
Norwegian Dance _____ E. Grieg
Rakoczy March _____ Czermak
Halls of Mountain King ____ E. Grieg
Solveig's Chant _____ E. Grieg
To Spring _____ E. Grieg
Asa's Death _____ E. Grieg
Hungarian Lustpiel _____ Keler-Bela
Selection, Flying Dutchman___Wagner
Temple Dance _____ E. Grieg
Lutheran Hymn _____ Luther

EXECUTIVE STAFF

Geo. A. Edes _____ Acting Manager
Branch O'Brien ____ Business Manager
Charles J. Oxley _____ Representative
Frederick A. Browne __Stage Manager
Theo. L. Currie _____ Musical Director
Frank Garrison ____ Master Mechanic
James Tague ____ Master of Properties
Charles Miller ____ Chief Electrician

8

George Primrose's All Star Minstrels

137

SUNDAY, MARCH 3

GEORGE PRIMROSE'S ALL STAR MINSTRELS

Presenting the Distinctly Original Idea

THE TEMPLE OF MIRTH AND MELODY

Introducing the following leading exponents of present day minstrelsy:

COMEDIANS

George Primrose, Neal Abel, Emile Subers, Eddie Horan.

PAGE FOUR.

PROGRAM — (Continued)

VOCALISTS
Will Oakland, David Irwin, Joe Birnes,
Jack Sample, Al Pine, Eugene Kelly,
Sam West, Will Watkins, Jack Clarke.

INTERLOCUTOR
David Irwin.

PART 1.
(This program is subject to slight
change.)

PAGE FIVE.

PROGRAM — (Continued)

Opening overture, including the famous
negro melodies of the past.
(Arranged by Charles Prokop.)
Laughing song and eccentric dance....
.... Eddie Horan
The Bell in the Light House..........
.... Jack Sample
The Last Rose of Summer is the Sweet-
est Song of All...............Sam West
I'd Rather Be Outside Looking In
Than Inside Looking Out ....Neal Abel

Hot and cold sodas, hot chocolate,
hot beef tea, hot lemonade, or in fact
any soft drink known.—Leon.

Everything new and up-to-date at F.
J. Munds.

PAGE SIX.

PROGRAM — (Continued)

While I Eave You..............Joe Birnes
I've Said My Last Farewell............
.... Emile Subers
When the Evening Breeze Is Sighing
.... David Irwin
Waltz Me, Bill ,...GEORGE PRIMROSE
Silver Threads Among the Gold—My
  Gal Sal..................... Will Oakland

Get the Habit—A Trip to Leon's After the Show.

Diamonds, watches, jewelry, cut glass—F. J. Mund's.

PAGE SEVEN.

PROGRAM — (Continued)

The first part will conclude with an original musical "recital" by Mme. Rascally's band, composed of the following soloists: Drummer, J. Burke; bass, drum, Steve Grady; cymbals, H. Dixon; trombone, Eddy Horan; Mme. Rascally, Neal Abel.

Intermission of about ten minutes. The Primrose song book on sale during intermission.

PAGE NINE.

142

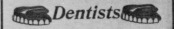

PROGRAM — (Continued)

PART II.

DRILL OF THE SOUTHERN CADETS.

A series of military evolutions arranged by Mr. Primrose, introducing the song, "Good Bye, Glory." David Irwin, captain.

PAGE TEN.

PROGRAM — (Continued)

GEORGE PRIMROSE

America's most graceful dancer, in a
melange of his world famous dances:
1. "By the Light of the Honeymoon."
2. "Twilight on the Old Plantation."
"Lazy Moon." 3. "De Essence of
Old Virginia." 4. Solo dance by Mr.
Primrose.

PAGE ELEVEN.

PROGRAM — (Continued)

The Original Georgia Sunflower
EMILE SUBERS
Singing Comedian.

TROCADERO QUARTETTE
Joe Birnes, Al Pine, Sam West, Jack
Samples. Individual vocalists and col-
lective harmonists.

Everything purchased at Munds is
guaranteed—I am here to stay.

PAGE THIRTEEN

SAVOY THEATER

122—STATE STREET—122

GOLDMAN & QUEROLLI, PROPS.

IKE GOLDMAN, Manager.

SHOW EVERY EVENING

NOTHING BUT FIRST CLASS AT-TRACTIONS.

PROGRAM.

THE SILVER SHOWER CLOG DANCE
Introducing Eddie Horan in his orig-inal walking clog..
Eugene Kelly, Ed Girton, J. E. Burke, J. Marlowe, Harry Lewis, Steve Grady, Barley Bros., Harland Dixon, Will Pack-ard.

THE MAGNOLIA HOTEL.
A burlesque on rural hotel life.
CAST OF CHARACTERS.
Proprietor of the hotel......David Irwin
Jay Coates .... Will Watkins
Mrs. Tottie Coughdrop..........J. Malone
"Front" .... John Burke
Silent Stillwalker ....Ed Horan
Mr. Tottie Coughdrop........John Bailey
—and—
The Duke of Pretzelburg......Neal Abel

Get the Habit—A Trip to Leon's After the Show.

Diamonds, watches, jewelry, cut glass —F. J. Mund's.

PAGE FOURTEEN.

PROGRAM — (Continued)

EXECUTIVE STAFF FOR MR. PRIM-
ROSE.

General Manager ....F. J. Dunne
General Agent ....John Coutts
Advertising Agent .... Will Riley
Stage Manager ....Will Oakland
Musical Director.............Chas. Prokop
Master Machinist........Henry Ackerman
Assistant Carpenter...........James Bass
Electrician .... Peter Winn

PAGE FIFTEEN.

ELKS OPERA HOUSE.
LEADVILLE Colo.

GEO. W. CASEY..................................Manager
F. E. RANDALL...............................Treasurer
JOE TAGART..............................Stage Manager
Booking Under Direction of Peter McCourt.

RULES AND INFORMATION.

Doors will be open at 7:45 p. m. Curtain will rise at 8:30 p. m.

The box office for the reservation of seats and boxes will open four days previous to each performance at 8 o'clock a. m at the Davis Drug Co corner Sixth and Harrison avenue. When buying seats be sure and look at the day. No mistakes can be rectified at the box office.

Tickets set aside for a performance and not called for by 2 p. m. on day of performance will be sold.

Persons arriving after the commencement of the performance will not be seated until the end of the act.

The management will esteem it a favor if patrons will remain seated until the final fall of the curtain, and requests that' the adjusting of hats and wraps may be deferred until the program is quite finished.

Ladies' retiring room and toilet will be found to the left. Check room for wraps, etc., will be found to the right. No charge will be made for checking.

Physicians and others anticipating calls during the performance should leave their seat location and name at the door., otherwise we cannot be held responsible for patrons not receiving same

The management requests that ladies will kindly not wear their hats in any part of the theater

"The Red Mill"

PROGRAM

TUESDAY, MAY 17, 1910.

MATRIN & EMERY COMPANY

Presents the Musical Comedy
Success

'THE RED MILL'

By Henry Blossom & Victor Herbert
Authors and Composers of "Mlle.
Modiste," "The Prima Donna," etc.

CAST OF CHARACTERS

Two Americans Doing Europe.

Con Kidder .... Bert O. Swor
Kidd Conner .... Franker Woods

PROGRAM—(Continued)

Jan Van Borken, Burgomaster of
 Katwk-ann-zee .... Otto Koerner
Franz, Sheriff of Katwk-ann-zee
.... Alvin Laughlin
Wilhelm, keeper of the Red Mill
 Inn .... Carl Hartberg
Capt. Dorris Van Damm, in love
with Gretchen .... S. W. Scott
The Governor of Zeeland, engaged
 to Gretchen ...... Harry R. McLain
Joshua Pennefeather, solisitor, Lin-
 coln's Inn Fields, London ....
.... Percy Bacon
Gretchen, the Burgomaster's dau-
 ghter .... Mabel de Nordendorf
Bertha, the Burgomasters sister ...
.... Jessie Houston

149

PROGRAM—(Continued)

Tina, barmaid, Wilhelm's daughter
.... Vernice Martyn
Countess de la Terre, automobiling
  with her sons through Holland...
.... Fay Adams

Flower Girls

Lena	Alice Vernice
Dora	Mabel Vanmeter
Anna	Opal Cole
Cora	Grace Bacon
Flora	Bonner Woods
Mina	Etta Stewart

Dahghters of Joshua Pennefeather

Alice	Zoe Brown
Cecil	Kathleen Primrose
Margueritte	Edith Edwards
Virgil	Lillian Putnam

TAKE ME TO
Miller's after the Show

PROGRAM—(Continued)

Notary	Weldon Sears
Butler	Emil Minet
Jocco, the Monk	By Himself

Peasants, Artists, Aide de Camp,
  Burghers, Fishers, etc.

Fifth Avenue Girls—The Misses
Adams, Vernice, Cole Stewart.

Broadway Girls—The Misses Yates,
Woods, Van Meter, Primrose.

Bowery Girls and Dutch Boys—
The Misses Collins, Putnam, Yates,
Cole.

Servants—The Misses Irving, Jewell, Putnam, Adams, Stewart, Cole,
Primrose, Festa, Price, Textrude.

Market Women—The Misses Forbes, Yates, Jewell, Primrose, Van
Meter.

150

PROGRAM—(Continued)

Fishwives—The Misses Adams, Collins, Cole, Stewart.

French Sons — Messrs. Phillips, Mack, Edwards, Domke.

Artists—Messrs. Wright, Collins, Miller, Phillips, Mack, Edwards.

Servants — Messrs. Roy, Miller, Price, Collins, Sears, Butler.

Aides—Messrs. Collins, Sears, Price, Miller, Roy, Williams.

Fishermen—Messrs. Collins, Roy, Sears, Price.

The Dutch Kiddies—Clarence and Elizabeth Johnson, Thomas, Jack, Peatta and Lorine Harrington.

Time—The Present   Place—Katwk-ann-zee.

PROGRAM—(Continued)

PROGRAM—(Continued)

MUSICAL NUMBERS
ACT I

1 Opening Chorus ....
.... Artists and Flower Girls
2 Migonette, Tina and Flower Girls
3 You Never Can Tell About a
Woman, Burgomaster and Wilhelm
4 Whistle It ....
.... Kidder, Conner and Tina
5 The Isle of Our Dreams ....
.... Gretchen and Capt .Dorris
6 Go, While the Goin's Good ....
.... Bertha, Tina, Conner and Kidder
7 When the World Is Fair ....
.... Ensemble
8 Monbeams Gretchen and Quartette
9 Finale   Gretchen and Quartette

Don't forget that J. ?. Miller is open
After the Show

ACT II

1 Opening Chorus ....
2 The Legend of the Mill ....
.... Bertha and House Maids
3 Good-a-Bye-John ....
.... Conner and Kidder
4 Love But You ....Tina and Tourists
5 Every Day is Ladies' Day With
Me .... Governor ond Aides
6 Because You're You ...... Bertha,
the Governor and Dutch Kiddies
7 In Old New York ....
.... Conner and Kidder
8 Wedding Bells .... Ensemble
9 Finale.
Music under the direction of
Lawrence Murray.
Chaperone .... Mme. Farley

PROGRAM—(Continued)

Last Act—Russet Brown is not the name of a man, but of the new color cloth now being used by Maurice Stiefel, The Man on the Spot, in his third season Klassy Klothes. The place to see for yourself is at 615 Tribune building, the Home of Individuality.

Costumes designed by Wilhelm of London. The modern dresses by Lord & Taylor, New York. The Scenery by Gates & Morange, New York, and constructed by T. Bernard McDonald, New York Shoes by Cammeyer, New York. Wigs by McDonald. Electrical equipment furnished by the Globe Equipment Company. Delft designs by the Delft Company. Properties by William Camph.

For a Bowl of Chili Go to Miller's

154

GEO. W. CASEY_____Manager
F. E. RANDALL_____Treasurer
JOE TAGART_____Stage Manager
(Booking under direction of Peter McCourt.)
DIRECTORS LEADVILLE ELKS BUILDING
ASSOCIATION
A. V. BOHN_____President
A. LUMSDEN_____Vice President
GEO W. CASEY_____Secretary-Treasurer
Chas. Cavender, E. J. McCarty, Geo. R. Becker, C. E.
Dickinson, I. L. Jones, K. L. Fahnestock.

RULES AND INFORMATION.

Doors will be open at 7:45 p. m. Curtain will rise
at 8:30 p. m.

The box office for the reservation of seats and
boxes will open four days previous to each performance
at 8 o'clock a. m. at the Davis Drug Co., corner Sixth
and Harrison Avenue.

Tickets set aside for a performance and not called
for by 2 p. m. on day of performance will be sold.

Persons arriving after the commencement of the performance will not be
seated until the end of the act.

The management will esteem it a favor if patrons will remain seated until
the final fall of the curtain, and requests that the adjusting of hats and wraps
may be deferred until program is quite finished.

Any difficulty arising in respect to errors in tickets or sittings should be
referred to the management for speedy and proper adjustment.

Ladies' retiring room and toilet will be found to the left. Check room for
wraps, etc., will be found to the right. No charge will be made for checking.

Physicians and others anticipating calls during the performance should
leave their seat location and name at the door.

The management requests that ladies will kindly not wear their hats in
any part of the theater.

"The Rivals"

155

PROGRAM—Continued.

CAST OF CHARACTERS

Sir Lucius O'Trigger _____
_____ Mr. Joseph W. Jefferson
"Bob" Acres _____
_____ Mr. William W. Jefferson
Sir Anthony Absolute _____
_____ Mr. T. C. Hamilton
Captain Absolute (under the assum-
ed name of Beverly) _____
_____ Mr. Leopold Lane
David _____ Mr. Philip Bishop
Falkland _____ Mr. George Germane
Fag _____ Mr. Serena Bonnie
Mrs. Malaprop _____ Miss Rosa Rand
Lydia Languish__Miss Blanche Bender
Lucy _____ Miss Mary Redmayne

HOFFMAN'S TOGGERY
30 per cent DISCOUNT SALE
IS ON

PROGRAM—Continued.

Manager _____ S. W. Donalds
Business Manager ____ Albert Dorris

The management earnestly requests and sincerely hopes that the audience will remain seated until the fall of the final curtain in order that the beautiful epilogue, written by the late Joseph Jefferson, may be heard to the fullest possible adantage and without the annoying and distracting features incidental to early departures.

$5.00 DOMESTIC COAL

MIDLAND COAL & COKE CO.
TELEPHONE 191

222 WEST CHESTNUT STREET
Order a Ton of Coal and get a Long Handled Dust Pan

PROGRAM—Continued.

FRIDAY, JANUARY 1, 1909
Mr. H. H. Frazee Presents

JAS. J. CORBETT

—IN—

FACING THE MUSIC

By James Henry Darnley. Staged by Mr. Willard Mack.

Poor Ben!

Up Against It Again!

Diamonds!
Watches!
Jewelry!

33⅓% DISCOUNT

BEN COHN & BROTHER
412 Harrison Avenue

The Saratoga

HOWARD GRISWOLD, Prop.
P. O. Box 593
LEADVILLE, COLORADO

See—The finest collection of mounted Heads in the city
Drop in after the play

DIAMONDS

33⅓ per Cent Off

Ben Cohn & Bro.
412 Harrison Avenue

PROGRAM—Continued.

THOSE CONCERNED.

John Smith, who owns race horses and stays out nights__Jas. J. Corbett
Rev. John Smith, the curate of St. Andrew's _____ Corwin Luskmoor
Dick Desmond, a friend of Smith__ _____ Jos. I. Sullivan
Col. Dudley Smith, John Smith's uncle _____ Geo. C. Denton
Sargt. Duffel, from Vine street ____ _____ Chas. Horn
Mrs. Ponting, the housekeeper ____ _____ Mae Dudley
Flora Featherly, of the Bijou theater _____ Lillian Logan
Nora _____ Amanda Hendricks
Mabel _____ Eleanor Montell

After the Entertainment

PROGRAM—Continued.

WHERE IT ALL OCCURS

Place—England.

Time—Right Now.

The action of the play takes place in John Smith's flat, No. 19 Mona, Mansions, Kensington.

PROGRAM—Continued.

SYNOPSIS

Between Acts I and II—Ten minutes.

Between Acts II and III—Ten minutes.

EXECUTIVE STAFF

Frank C. Rhoades _____, Manager
Geo. B. Hunt _____ Business Manager
Chas. Horn _____ Stage Manager
Harry A. Miller _____ Carpenter

163

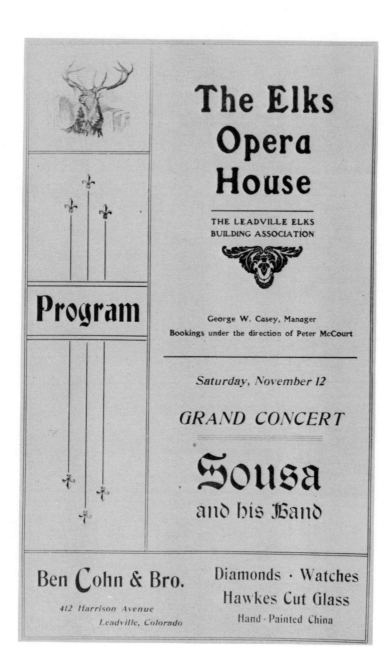

John Philip Sousa & His Band

The H. H. Tomkins Hardware Co.

WHOLESALE AND RETAIL

HARDWARE

Mine and Smelter Supplies

CORNER HARRISON AVENUE AND FIFTH STREET, LEADVILLE

—THE—

Leadville Dancing Academy

OTIS A. RICHMOND,
PROPRIETOR

ARMORY HALL
East Fifth Street

Lessons and Social Hop every **Tuesday** and **Saturday** evenings Lessons from 8:30 to 9:30. Social from 9:30 to 12 P. M.

Children's class every Saturday afternoon.

All the Latest Dances taught. Private lessons a specialty.

Hall and Music furnished for Dancing Parties and Balls The best floor in the city.

Admission, 50 cents.
Ladies Free.

Lodge Room for rent, can accommodate large or small lodges.

INFORMATION.

Doors open at 7:45. Curtain rises 8:30. The box office for the reservation of seats and boxes will open four days previous to each performance at 8 o'clock a. m. at George W. West's cigar store in the Elks' Opera House Block.

Regular patrons may have the same seats reserved for each performance. If not called for by 2 o'clock on day of performance they will be sold. Failure to call for seats for three performances in succession will forfeit the right to same in future.

Ladies' retiring room and toilet will be found to the left.

Check room for wraps, umbrellas, etc., will be found to the right. No charge will be made or checking articles.

The curtain rises promptly at 8:30. The regular patrons know this, and as a rule come in time to be seated. The very numerous complaints from all sides have forced the management to adopt a rule in regard to late comers, and such positively cannot be seated while curtain is up. While this may seem a hardship on the few, it is the only way, and in order to be seated and enjoy the first act it will be absolutely necessary to get into the house not later than 8:25.

Physicians and others anticipating calls during the performance should leave their seat location with the usher.

The management requests that ladies will kindly not wear their hats in any part of the theatre.

CHILDREN—Children in arms positively not admitted to theatre.

Ladies having in charge children who become noisy will be expected to promptly remove them from the theatre.

SILVER STATE RESTAURANT

THE ONLY
First - Class
SHORT ORDER
RESTAURANT
IN THE CITY

※

220
Harrison Avenue

※

MARTINELLI & CO.

167

Kodaks & Kodak Supplies

We sell you a Kodak, teach you how to take and develop pictures, so that you can take all kinds of pictures at a very little expense

Nicolai's Pharmacy, Leadville

Saturday, Nov. 12

GRAND CONCERT

— BY —

Sousa and His Band

Program for the Evening
(9 o'clock.)

1. Overture, "William Tell..........Rossini

2. Cornet Solo, "Valse Brilliante"..Clarke
   Mr .Herbert L. Clarke.

3. Suite, "At the King's Court" (new)..
   ....Sousa
   (a) "Her Grace, the Duchess."
   (b) "Her Ladyship, the Countess."
   (c) "Her Majesty, the Queen "

Blue Delph, at the American Jewelry Company.

(5)

SOUSA AND HIS BAND.

4. Aria for Soprano, Nightingale air from "The Marriage of Jeannette"......
....Masse..
Miss Estelle Liebling.
Flute Obligato by Mr .Marshall Lufsky.

5. Processional of the Knights of the Grail from "Parsifal".....Wagner
"Oh food forever blessed, God's gift from day to day,
In prayer to him addressed, for life and strength we pray;
As anguished and lowly, the Savior Holy, His life for us did offer,
So in deep contrition and glad submission, to Him now our all we proffer."

Intermission.

Carving sets, at the American Jewelry Company.

(6)

SOUSA AND HIS BAND.

6. American Character Sketches (new)
....E. R. Kroeger
  (a) "The Gamin."
  (b) "An Indian Lament."
  (c) "Voodoo Night Scene"
  (d) "The Dancing Darkey"

7. (a) Melody "To a Wild Rose" from
    Woodland Sketches" (new).........
    ....McDowell
  (b) March, "Jack Tar"....... ....Sousa

8. Violin Solo, "Zigeunerweisen".Sarasate
    Miss Jessie Straus.

9. Overture, "Poet and Peasant"....Suppe

We do emblem and badge work at the
American Jewelry Company.

(7)

GEO. W. CASEY,
Manager.

F. E. RANDALL,
Treasurer.

ELKS OPERA HOUSE

Program Publisher,
JOHN W. BARRETT.

Booking Under the Direction of
PETER McCOURT.

BILL OF THE PLAY

FRIDAY NIGHT, JULY 20, 1906.

THE FAMOUS
ARINGTON'S COMEDIANS

Presenting the Greatest Temperance
Drama ever written, in Five Acts.

TEN NIGHTS IN A BARROOM

CAST OF CHARACTERS.

Sample Swichel.........W. W. Craig

Simon Slade..............U. S. Allen

Joe Morgan...............A. J. Cole

Frank Slade..........Arthur Walton

Harvey Green........Thomas Pawley

Willie Hamond..........Lew Virden

William Romaine...Maurice Francillon

Mrs. Slade..............Elsa Morgan

Mrs. Morgan..........Florence Craig

Mary Morgan...........Little Helen

Mehitabel Cartwright, Mayme Arington

"Come dear friend, to Leon's Ice
Cream and Soda Water Parlors, nothing he sells will hurt you."

Don't Forget the Social Hop, Tuesday and Saturday nights at Joyce's
Dancing Academy.

The furniture used on the stage is
from the J. W. Smith Dry Goods and
Household Furnishing Co.

SYNOPSIS.

Act I.—Sickle and Sheaf. Interview
betwen Romaine and the Yankee. Poor
old Joe, the inebriate. Little Mary in
search of her father. Quarrel between
Green and Willie. Timely arrival of the
Yankee.

Act II.—The Yankee and the philanthropist. The landlord's enterprising
son, Frank. Quarrel between the landlord and his drunken customer. The
bottle and the fatal blow. Arrival of
little Mary. "Father, they have killed
me!"

Act III.—The Yankee and the gambler. The treat. The drunkard's home.
The patient wife by the side of her suffering child. Joe Morgan's promise.
"Come, dear father, this is little Mary's
room; nothing can hurt you here."

Act IV.—The Sickle and the Sheaf.
Landlord and son. Fight and death of
Willie Hamond. The arrest. "I'll
never drink another drop as long as I
live." The dream of little Mary.

Act V.—The meeting of Sample and
Romaine after an absence of five years.
Appearance of Simon Slade. The happy
home of Morgan. The Wife's joy.
Sample and his new suit.

Don't Forget the Social Hop, Tuesday and Saturday nights at Joyce's
Dancing Academy.

The furniture used on the stage is
from the J. W. Smith Dry Goods and
Household Furnishing Co.

Have you ever tried one of Leon's
Plain or Ice Cream Sodas after the
show? If not, why not?

---

*"Ten Nights In A Barroom;" "A California Detective;" and "Under Two
Flags."*

PROGRAM.

SATURDAY NIGHT, JULY 21, 1906.

THE FAMOUS ARINGTON'S COMEDIANS

Will Present the Great Sensational
Comedy Drama in Four Acts,

A CALIFORNIA DETECTIVE

or, RISEN FROM THE ASHES.

CAST OF CHARACTERS.

Gerald Grey..............W. W. Craig
Joe Blossom . . . . .W. W. Craig
Lester Blake, a villain from choice,
. . . . .U. S. Allen
Mosher, a Jew............Lew Virden
Jack Furbish, a detective and re-
porter, ...Thomas Pawley
Michel O'Connell............A. J. Cole
Mr. Wilson..........M. A. Francillon
Ike Parsons, a bartender...F. Emmons
Mr. Pidgeon, a faro dealer...J. Frazer
James................ ....Edwin Adair
Blanche, the orange girl.....
. . . . .Florence Craig
Ella La Fluer, actress.............
. . . . :...........Florence Craig
Flora Blake, Lester's sister.......
. . . . .Elsa Morgan
Kittie Loraine, a premier danseuse,
. . . .Mayme Arington

Don't Forget the Social Hop, Tuesday and Saturday nights at Joyce's
Dancing Academy.

172

PROGRAM.

SYNOPSIS.

Act I.—Scene 1: Lester Blake's
home, New Orleans. Scene 2: Street
in New Orleans. Scene 3: Attic in old
tenement house on Padryes street. The
great fire scene.

Act II.—A lapse of three years.
Scene 1: Street in New Orleans. Scene
2: Lester Blake's house. Scene 3:
Street. Scene 4: Lester Blake's gam-
bling house. Joe Blossom, right from
California.

Act III.—Scene 1: Street in New
Orleans. Scene 2: Ella La Fluer's
apartments. Scene 3: Street. Scene 4:
Old saloon on Water street.

Act IV.—Scene 1: Street. Scene 2:
Lester Blake's home. Always be sure
of your point before you show your
hand.

Always be sure of your drink before
you raise your hand.—Mine Host Leon

The furniture used on the stage is
from the J. W. Smith Dry Goods and
Household Furnishing Co.

If you are contemplating give a ball,
social, card party or any private or
public entertainment where you need a
hall, be sure and see Professor Joyce.

PROGRAM.

SUNDAY NIGHT, JULY 22, 1906.

Under Two Flags

CAST OF CHARACTERS.

Bertie Cecil, known as Louis Victor, ...Thomas Pawley
Berkeley Cecil, his brother........
.... Maurice Francillon
Lord Rockingham, known as the Seraph.................U. S. Allen
Rake, an Irish Knight of the Pigskin.............W. W. Craig
Col. Chateuray, called the Black Hawk.................A. J. Cole
Ben Davis, a tout..........J. Frazer
Baroni, Jew money lender..Lew Virden
Capt. Leroux, a trooper..Geo. Saunders
Petit Picpon, a trooper....Frank Mills
Pierre Maton, a trooper, Arthur Walton
Veneita, Rockingham's sister, afterwards Princess Corona Elsa Morgan
Lady Guenevere........Florence Craig
Nora McShane, Venetia's maid...
....Miss Edwards
Cigarette, the friend of the Flag,
....Mayme Arington

SYNOPSIS.

Act 1—England. Epsom Downs. The race The forged note. Steeplechase for life.
Act 2—Algiers. After 12 years. Arrival of Cigarette. A Soldier of France.
Act 3—Nest of the Silver Pheasant. The blow. "You lie and you know you lie!"
Act 4—Interval of 2 days. Hour before sunset.. "I'm ready; give your signal." Cigarette! France! Death of Cigarette.

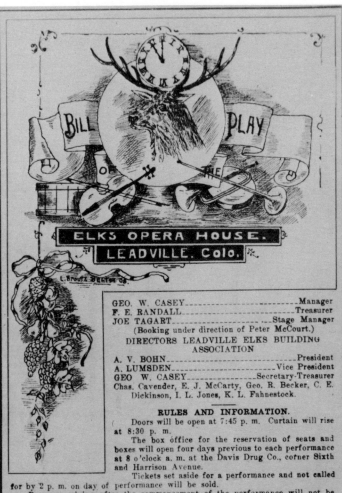

BILL OF THE PLAY

ELKS OPERA HOUSE.
LEADVILLE, Colo.

GEO. W. CASEY_____Manager
F. E. RANDALL_____Treasurer
JOE TAGART_____Stage Manager
(Booking under direction of Peter McCourt.)
DIRECTORS LEADVILLE ELKS BUILDING
ASSOCIATION
A. V. BOHN_____President
A. LUMSDEN_____Vice President
GEO W. CASEY_____Secretary-Treasurer
Chas. Cavender, E. J. McCarty, Geo. R. Becker, C. E.
Dickinson, I. L. Jones, K. L. Fahnestock.

RULES AND INFORMATION.

Doors will be open at 7:45 p. m. Curtain will rise
at 8:30 p. m.

The box office for the reservation of seats and
boxes will open four days previous to each performance
at 8 o'clock a. m. at the Davis Drug Co., corner Sixth
and Harrison Avenue.

Tickets set aside for a performance and not called
for by 2 p. m. on day of performance will be sold.

Persons arriving after the commencement of the performance will not be
seated until the end of the act.

The management will esteem it a favor if patrons will remain seated until
the final fall of the curtain, and requests that the adjusting of hats and wraps
may be deferred until program is quite finished.

Any difficulty arising in respect to errors in tickets or sittings should be
referred to the management for speedy and proper adjustment.

Ladies' retiring room and toilet will be found to the left. Check room for
wraps, etc., will be found to the right. No charge will be made for checking.

Physicians and others anticipating calls during the performance should
leave their seat location and name at the door.

The management requests that ladies will kindly not wear their hats in
any part of the theater.

"The Toymaker"

PROGRAM—Continued.

CAST OF CHARACTERS

The Toymaker .... Teddy Webb
His Wife .... Aimee Leicester
Elsie, his daughter .. Daphne Pollard

2

PROGRAM—Continued.

Francois, serving an apprenticeship
in the monastry .... Eugene Wiener
Ollendorf, uncle of Francois
.... Al Wilder

Diamonds, watches, jewelry, cut glass
- F. J. Mund's

179

PROGRAM—Continued.

Bachenswartz, friend of Ollendorf's
————————— Frank Bertrand
Notary Public ———— Chas. Browning

Diamonds, watches, jewelry, cut glass
—F. J. Mund's

5

180

PROGRAM—Continued.

Workmen in the Toy Shop—
    Robert _____ Clara Merek
    Henry _____ Jas. Browning
    Jackey _____ Arthur Ray

6

After the Entertainment

finish the evening with a refreshing, thirst quenching glass or two of "Columbine Beer." It's astonishing how it sets one up without the least feeling of discomfort in the morning. If you will taste it we won't need to tell you how palatable "Columbine Beer" is.

PROGRAM—Continued.

Loucy .... Anna Chapman
Schmidt .... Mabel Hilliard
August .... Pearl Girard

Chimes used in first act made by Los Angeles Musical Co.

7

PROGRAM—Continued.

SYNOPSIS OF SCENES

ACT I—Scene 1—The Monastry. Scene 2—The Toy Shop.

ACT II—Scene 1—Reception Room. Count Ballenberg's Castle. Scene 2—The Monastry.

8

Scenes

Scene from The Toymaker, Land of Nod

Scene from "Mam'selle Napoleon"

Scene from "The Beauty Spot"

Scene from "The Forbidden Land" photo by The Geo. R. Lawrence Co., Chicago.

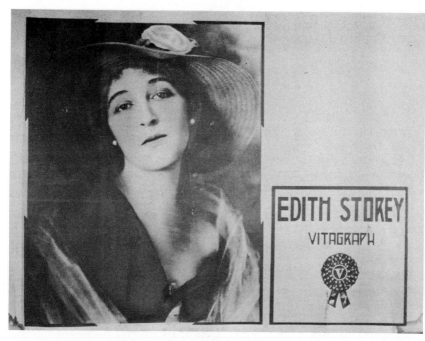

Edith Story. From original poster at The Tabor Opera House.

Poster scene from ''Aladdin From Broadway'' at The Tabor Opera House.

PRODUCTIONS, AT RANDOM

Circa

1879-1910

Across the Desert; Alexander, the Great; Arizona; As You Like It; Around the World in Eighty Days; At Cripple Creek; At the Old Cross Roads.

The Banker's Daughter; Beau Brummel; The Beauty Spot; The Black Flag; Bohemian Girl; Bonnie Brier; The Bonnie Brier Bush; The Burglar's Child.

Camille; A Chinese Honeymoon; Chocolate Soldier; Chimes of Normandy; Clews; The Coleen Baun; A Comedy of Errors; Cordelia's Aspirations; The County Chairman; The Country Detective; Cousin Kate; The Curfew Shall Not Ring Tonight.

David Harum; Davy Crockett; Deborah; Deception; Devil's Auction; Don Caesar De Bazan.

Eben Holden; The Embezzler; Enoch Arden; Esmeralda.

Fanchon, the Cricket; Figaro; Florodora; The Four Cohens; Francisca Da Rimini; French Spy; A Friend of the Family; Fun on the Bristol.

The Gay Parisians; The Great Strike; Grimes Cellar Door; Gypsy Baron.

Haddon Hall; Hamlet; Hazel Kirke; Held by the Enemy; A Heroine in Rags; The Hills of California; His Absent Boy; Hobbies; Hooligan's Troubles; Human Hearts.

In Old Tennessee; Isle of Spice.

A Jolly American Tramp; Julius Caesar.

Kerry Gow.

Lady Audley's Secret; The Lady of Lyons; The Land of Nod; Leah, The Jewish Maiden; Lena, the Madcap; Life and Trials of a Factory Girl; The Little Minister; Little Nell; London Assurance; Lost in New York.

Macbeth; Maj. Wellington De Boots; Mam'selle Napoleon; The Man in a Maze; Man of the People; Marie Antoinette; Mary Stuart; The Matchmaker; Mazeppa; The Merry Widow; A Message from Mars; The Middleman; A Midsummer Night's Dream; Monsieur Beaucaire; A Mountain Pink; My Little Partner; My Son-in-Law.

New East Lynne.

The Octroon; Old Curiousity Shop; Old Lavender; The Old Homestead; Oliver Twist; On the Bridge at Midnight; Othello; Our Bachelors; Our Boarding House; Our New Minister.

Parsifal; The Passion Play; Phoenix; Pinafore; The Pit; Polly of the Circus; The Power of Love; Pretty Peggy; The Princess Chic; The Princess of Patches.

Ranson's Folly; The Red Mill; Richelieu; Richard the Third; Rip van Winkle; The Rivals; Robin Hood; A Romance in Ireland; Rosemary; The Runaways; Rupert of Hentzau.

Salammbo; San Toy; Sapho; Secret Service; She; Shaugraun; Sharps and Flats; Shore Acres; The Show Girl; Sis Hopkins; The Silver Slipper; State's

Evidence; A Stranger in a Strange Land; Streets of New York; Sunny Side of Broadway; Sweet Clover.

The Tatooed Man; The Temple of Music and Laughter; Ten Nights in a Barroom; A Texas Steer; Theodora; The Tie That Binds; The Time, The Place and the Girl; A Trip to Egypt; Trodden Down; Two Orphans; Two Little Waifs.

Uncle Tom's Cabin; Under Southern Skies.

The Virginian.

Way Down East; When Knighthood Was in Flower; The Witching Hours; Wolves of New York; The World; Wyoming.

York State Folks; Yon Yonson.

Zaza; Zillah, The Hebrew Mother.

THE END.

Evelyn E. Livingston Furman
Leadville, Colorado
1972.